ENGLISH EXERCISES FOR SECRETARIES

ENGLISH EXERCISES FOR SECRETARIES

By

R. A. KELLY B.A.

LECTURER AT KINGSTON TECHNICAL COLLEGE

GEORGE G. HARRAP & CO. LTD
LONDON   TORONTO   WELLINGTON   SYDNEY

First published in Great Britain 1959
by GEORGE G. HARRAP & CO. LTD
182 High Holborn, London, W.C.1

Reprinted: 1959; 1960

COMPOSED IN BASKERVILLE TYPE AND PRINTED AT THE PITMAN PRESS, BATH
MADE IN GREAT BRITAIN

PREFACE

THIS text-book is intended to guide the student who has already taken a general course in English towards the more limited technique of English for business. It is obvious that a secretary or shorthand-typist should have a sound practical knowledge of the language, but she must also learn to view it in a new light. A leisurely, academic approach is not suited to the demands and tempo of business life, where speed and accuracy are of paramount importance. High shorthand speeds are of doubtful value if transcriptions contain errors of grammar, punctuation, or spelling. Ninety per cent accuracy is not sufficient, and accuracy of the slow, plodding type is out of place.

The exercises in this book are designed to help develop speed and accuracy within the limits of commercial work, and with a view to correlation with the basic commercial skills. Many of the exercises can be used as practical typing or dictation tests, and it is hoped that they will prove useful to the teacher who has to deal with both shorthand typewriting and English.

The author has tried to preserve a balance between the teacher's wish for sufficient exercises and the private student's demand for comment and guidance. It is hoped that the teacher can in this way supplement his individual approach to the subject with suitable references and practical work.

Where possible, the material is simple, without any attempt to introduce the more specialized forms of correspondence. The aim in the early stages of instruction should be to concentrate on the basic principles of composition, leaving specialization until later. Indeed, the attitude of many employers is summed up in the statement, "Teach them to be clear, concise, and accurate, and leave the special form and vocabulary to us."

Although designed for students working towards such examinations as the Royal Society of Arts Shorthand Typists' Certificate, the text contains material of wider application which should make it useful to the general student of commercial subjects.

ACKNOWLEDGEMENTS

FOR permission to use copyright extracts the author and publishers offer their grateful thanks to the following:

Penguin Books, Ltd, for extracts from *Education in England*, by W. Kenneth Richmond, *The Science of Seeing*, by I. Mann and A. Pirie, and *Film*, by Roger Manvell.

Messrs Routledge and Kegan Paul, Ltd, for an extract from *Technics and Civilization*, by L. Mumford.

The Royal Society of Arts, for extracts from several examination papers.

The office of *The Writer's and Artist's Year Book*, for an extract from *The Writer's and Artist's Year Book*.

The author would also like to acknowledge the helpful advice and criticism given by his colleagues in the Commerce Department of Kingston Technical College, particularly the help given by the Librarian, P. R. Brunning, A.L.A., in the compiling of the Reference section.

CONTENTS

SECTION I

VOCABULARY

A. Exercises in the Knowledge and Use of a Dictionary
B. Vocabulary and Context Exercises
C. Word-differentiation Lists
D. Standard and Common Phrases
E. Common Spelling Errors
F. Spelling Errors in Transcription
G. Supplementary Vocabulary and Spelling Lists
H. Abbreviations
I. Foreign Words and Phrases

A. Exercises in the Knowledge and Use of a Dictionary

1. Give a list of the types of information which may be obtained from a good dictionary.

2. Explain at least two limitations of a dictionary.

3. Why does a dictionary have to be revised and reprinted every so often?

4. Give five abbreviations used in explaining dictionary entries and indicate the significance of each.

5. What is meant by the 'derivation' of a word?

6. Explain two methods of indicating the correct pronunciation of a word.

7. What is the purpose of an addendum to a dictionary?

8. What types of foreign words and phrases will be found in most English dictionaries?

9. In a short paragraph, explain the following dictionary entry:

> **dense,** a. Closely compacted in substance; crowded together; crass, stupid. Hence *densely* adv., *denseness* n. (f. L. *densus*.)

10. Give a suitable dictionary definition for each of the following (compare your answer with an actual dictionary entry):

> bicycle   return (verb)   narrow (adj.)

11. Arrange the following in the order they would appear in a dictionary:

> reinstate   ac-   tyranny   purpose   re-
> in-   topaz   cardiac   rehearse   forthright
> perpendicular   restore   agree   restoration
> interest   house   cellular   optical   -ar
> machinery   rubber   porpoise

Refer to each in the *Concise Oxford Dictionary* and note carefully how they are explained. Pay particular attention to the prefixes and suffixes.

12. Explain the following dictionary entry:

> **-lite,** suf. forming names of minerals, (F, f. Gk *lithos* stone) usu. preceded by -o-.

13. Give a suitable dictionary definition for:

television   prepaid   renovate

14. Arrange the following in dictionary order:

litany   corrode   acclaim   furnish   apple
monetary   corrosion   level   furnace
application   redness   mess   corner   military
literature   accord   withstand   bath   occupy
eradicate

15. What other information is sometimes given in dictionary form?

16. Explain the following dictionary entry:

bob, v.i. Move up & down, rebound; curtsey; *b. up like a cork*, survive defeat. (etym. dub.)

17. Give the full form of the following abbreviations used in dictionary entries:

colloqu.   bibl.   Du.   fig.   Skr.
Hind.   suf.   obs.   O.T.   fol.

18. Arrange the following in dictionary order:

medulla   practise   *galimatias*   medley
galleon   meeting   *requiescat*   practice
meddle   waft   gallows   mediaeval
cyclist   stipulate   requisition   stipend
praemunire   cyclic   prairie   cyclone
request   stipple   wafer   galley
waif   cycle   require   sting
practical   medium

Why are certain of the words in italics?

19. What have the following words in common?

elephant   royal   brief   atlas   demy

20. Explain the following dictionary entry:

schedule (she-). n. & v.t. inventory, detailed list, appendix; make a list of, include in a detailed list. (M.E. *cedule*, f. L. for papyrus-strip)

B. **Vocabulary and Context Exercises**

Study carefully each sentence in the following exercises and express clearly the meaning of each of the words in italics.

Exercise 1

(a) The shoe manufacturers had been told by various people that their products were popular, but they were not satisfied with *oral* comments and waited for more *tangible* evidence from the sales *returns*.

(b) The workmen often complained about their hours but could not *cavil* at the new arrangements whereby fewer hours could be worked in return for higher *production*.

(c) The *criterion* of good manners is thoughtfulness for others.

(d) His defence was *plausible*, but the facts were not *corroborated* by witnesses.

(e) After his business had failed he was *sceptical* of advice given to him to start again.

(f) The sailor had a reputation for thoughtful *application* to duty, but he suddenly developed an *irrational* behaviour which gave rise to actions endangering the safety of his ship.

(g) Among criminals there seems to be a *tacit* agreement that one should not 'poach' upon the *preserves* of another.

(h) She proved to be a successful tennis player despite her *unorthodox* strokes.

(i) Despite his many misfortunes, the sick man *maintained* a *stoical* attitude which amazed his friends.

(j) To his *chagrin* the much coveted prize was awarded to a boy whom he considered to be well below him in *attainment*.

Exercise 2

(a) He gives as a reason for his late arrival the excuse that the directions were not sufficiently *explicit*.

(b) The new theory was much too *nebulous*, and the lecturer found it almost impossible to explain it simply to an audience of *laymen*.

(c) It would be *hypocritical* to pretend that I have any regard for him; his *fastidiousness* has always annoyed me.

(d) The fact that Johnny was always receiving larger helpings of dessert suggested that he was receiving *preferential* treatment.

(*e*) The old man's appeal to be allowed to remain in the *condemned* house aroused much sympathy, especially when it became known that the council had *summarily* dismissed his plea.

(*f*) He was advised to *relinquish* his post of economic adviser as he had revealed little *aptitude* for the job.

(*g*) The strong feeling he had against a particular section of society caused him to *digress* from the main theme of his speech and to give a *dissertation* on existing social evils.

(*h*) The proposal to grant *concessions* to a rival company for trade within a certain area was carried *unanimously*, but it was understood that a *stipulation* would be made that all representatives of that company would be required to produce proper *credentials*.

(*i*) The policeman's *judicious* action in removing the drunken man quickly and quietly was approved by all present.

(*j*) The *seniority* of the employee did not help him to gain promotion because he showed little *initiative*.

Exercise 3

(*a*) After a *scrupulous* examination of the evidence, the court came to the conclusion that the younger man had been *coerced* into effecting *fraudulent conversion*.

(*b*) Despite the high professional *status* of Mr Smith, it seemed that the voters were *prejudiced* in favour of a local candidate.

(*c*) After the *anomalous* Act had been *repealed*, Parliament was able to start afresh with attempts to provide a more *equitable* system of *legislation*.

(*d*) The two companies *amalgamated* in an attempt to cut production costs and several *associate* firms were *incorporated* as *subsidiary* companies.

(*e*) The injury which he had sustained *jeopardized* the refugee's chances of escaping the evil *machinations* of his *oppressors*.

(*f*) At an *extraordinary* meeting of the council a *resolution* concerning the use of certain building materials was *rescinded*.

(*g*) The *sociologist* led his research team in an *exhaustive* survey of family life in Britain.

(*h*) Perhaps it was because he was in an *expansive* mood that he distributed presents to his staff in an *unprecedented* manner.

(*i*) He was unpopular at work because of his *misanthropic* attitude, and people became weary of his curtness and his *saturnine* expression.

(*j*) An historian should *adopt* an *objective* attitude to his work and treat facts *impartially*.

Exercise 4

(*a*) He decided not to *stint* himself on holiday, but found that he had spent a *disproportionate* amount of his money on entertainment.

(*b*) The member of the Opposition was told that the new Order was *provisional* until such times as the results of the scheme could be carefully *analysed*.

(*c*) The most *intractable* boy in the class was a moody youngster with a *truculent* attitude towards his teachers.

(*d*) Although he had no *pretensions* to being an *accomplished* pianist, he was capable of providing good entertainment.

(*e*) People were annoyed at his *phlegmatic* nature and wished he would *evince* more enthusiasm.

(*f*) He was unable to *substantiate* his claim to the property and tried to *inveigle* the successful claimant into signing it away.

(*g*) He argued that his unkind action had been the result of a momentary mental *aberration* and not of *malice*.

(*h*) The *gravamen* of his charge was that the crime had been committed with the *connivance* of a responsible person in public service.

(*i*) The authorities announced that *sporadic* outbreaks of a new and rare disease had *incapacitated* many workers in essential industries.

(*j*) Lack of *cohesion* in his argument led to *misconstruction* of his ideas, and the organization lost many *adherents* who would have responded to an appeal by a person of greater *perspicacity*.

Exercise 5

(*a*) The general was *astute* since he realized quickly that, although each of his artillery bombardments would be *tactically* ineffective, the *cumulative* effect upon enemy *morale* would be enormous.

(*b*) He *interpolated* several *derogatory* remarks into the conversation, until the host, who was *susceptible* to adverse criticism, took offence at the *aspersions* that had been cast upon his character.

(*c*) His attempts to *disseminate* propaganda of a *subversive* nature *provoked* a great deal of hostility from the authorities.

(*d*) To many of the audience the speaker's remark was unnecessarily *facetious*, but those people who possessed some knowledge of the subject realized that it was a particularly *trenchant* comment.

(*e*) It was a *fallacious* argument based on *palpable* errors, and no one was deceived by the speaker's *eloquence*.

(*f*) The new members of the club were put at their ease by the *congenial* atmosphere.

(*g*) Even after a *cursory* glance at the vase the *connoisseur* was able to give his *candid* opinion that it was worthless.

(*h*) Although he was a man who had reached the *zenith* of his career, he *expropriated* company funds, a deed which must have been *actuated* by strange inner *promptings*.

(*i*) It was *disconcerting* for him to find that many of his carefully prepared plans had come to nothing, and he soon lost his *complacent* attitude.

(*j*) The committee were *chary* about going ahead with the vote of *censure* and agreed to postpone any action until it had received the *endorsement* of the general members.

C. Word-differentiation Lists

The following groups contain pairs of words that are similar in meaning, appearance, or sound and are often confused. Show the difference between the words in each pair by using them in sentences.

into	in to	error	fault
already	all ready	begin	start
sheer	shear	vary	differ
aught	ought	short	brief
revenge	avenge	ask	enquire
keep	retain	recall	recollect
old	ancient	respect	esteem
permit	consent	worry	anxiety

rout	route	confine	restrict
defer	differ	dense	solid
canvas	canvass	straight	strait
adverse	averse	prolong	extend
concise	precise	practice	practise
refuse	decline	custom	tradition
historic	historical	divert	diverge
reverse	converse	ceiling	sealing
unite	unify	practical	practicable
fateful	fatal	intense	intent
enquire	inquire	forceful	forcible
eminent	imminent	literal	literary
recover	re-cover	result	effect
alternate	alternative	advise	inform
intense	intensive	authentic	genuine
contrast	compare	piteous	pitiful
successful	lucky	observation	observance
insensible	insensitive	physical	psychical
uninterested	disinterested	proposal	proposition
discomfort	discomfiture	inconstant	inconsistent
credible	credulous	elementary	elemental
ambiguous	uncertain	tendency	inclination
instigate	incite	deficient	defective
impressive	impressionable	palate	palette
insoluble	insolvent	local	locale
imaginable	imaginary	impunity	immunity
precedent	precedence	necessary	necessitous
efficient	efficacious	cubical	cubicle
contemptible	contemptuous	lightening	lightning
sensuous	sensual	politic	political
deprecate	depreciate	respectfully	respectively
reverent	reverend	appropriate	expropriate

stimulus	stimulant	— obsolete	— obsolescent
imperial	imperious	elicit	illicit
vigorous	virile	virtual	virtuous
physician	physicist	presumptive	presumptuous
concur	coincide	unsatisfied	dissatisfied

D. Standard and Common Phrases

In each of the following exercises explain the phrases and use each of them correctly in a sentence.

1. common usage
   ample opportunity
   drastic methods
   popular sentiment
   superficial resemblance

   contrary to expectation
   press conference
   short-sighted policy
   easing the situation
   poetic licence

2. cumulative effect
   for practical purposes
   with legitimate pride
   satisfactory compromise
   mass observation

   moral welfare
   contemporary account
   showing the flag
   the golden mean
   bulk buying

3. dutiable goods
   passive resistance
   unassuming attitude
   patently obvious
   damn with faint praise

   delegated authority
   limited resources
   substantial alterations
   commercial transaction
   prevalent attitude

4. irreparable calamity
   on unimpeachable evidence
   division of labour
   excess profits
   official procedure

   authorized to negotiate
   literary convention
   standard work
   political controversy
   cursory examination

5. psychological moment
   incidental expenses
   official sanction
   leading question
   legal aspect

   constitutional crisis
   ingratiating behaviour
   diplomatic relations
   annual assessment
   breach of contract

6. uncompromising attitude   ostensible reason
   restrictive practices   acceptable formula
   categorical denial   retrograde step
   interested party   accredited representative
   subversive activity   fair comment

7. stringent regulations   significant detail
   extenuating circumstances   informed opinion
   definitive edition   indictable offence
   active participation   standard equipment
   material needs   pertinent remarks

8. frozen assets   abridged edition
   staple commodities   proprietary goods
   tacit agreement   unsolicited testimonial
   process of rehabilitation   recognizance work
   secondary poverty   statistical evidence

9. universal practice   substantive motion
   capital investment   allied products
   trading profit   increased turnover
   liquid resources   interim dividend
   gross income   redeemable stock

10. comprehensive policy   deferred annuity
    limited liability   assigned revenues
    comparative costing   unilateral action
    fiscal policy   credit restriction
    profit margin   capital commitments

E. **Common Spelling Errors**

The following alphabetical list contains words which some students either find difficult to spell or spell carelessly. If your spelling is weak, practise with groups of words from the list. Take extra time and care to master them, for your spelling must be one hundred per cent accurate.

| absence | accessible | achieve |
| acceptance | accommodate | acknowledge |

acquiesce
acquire
address
advisable
aerial
aggravate
agreeable
all right
allotted
amateur
anomaly
answer
Antarctic
anxiety
appalling
apparent
appearance
appropriate
argument
ascend
awful
bachelor
beginning
believe
benefited
Britain
business
campaign
category
ceiling
cemetery
circuit
commemorate
committee
comparative
competent
concession
concurrence
conscientious
conscious

consistent
courteous
criticism
decease
deceive
decision
deferred
definite
disappear
disappoint
disastrous
discernible
discipline
discreetly
dissatisfied
distinctive
efficient
eighth
eligible
eliminate
embarrassment
emphasize (s)
enrolment
enthusiasm
equipped
especially
essential
exaggerate
excellent
exercise
exhaust
existence
expense
extravagance
familiar
February
feign
financial
foreign
forestall

forfeit
formerly
forty
friend
gauge
gazetteer
government
grammar
gramophone
grievance
handkerchief
harassed
heaven
height
honorary
humorous
hygienic
hypocrisy
illegible
immediately
imminent
incidental
independent
indispensable
inflammable
influential
insistent
intelligent
irresistible
knowledge
leisure
lieutenant
lightning
lik(e)able
livelihood
lose
maintenance
manœuvre
marriage
meant

medicine	plausible	separate
Mediterranean	pleasant	sergeant
miniature	possess	shield
minutes	preceding	shining
miscellaneous	preferred	similar
mischievous	privilege	simultaneous
murmuring	procedure	sincerely
nauseous	proceeds	skilful
necessary	profession	speech
negligible	pronunciation	success
niece	proprietary	supersede
noticeable	psychology	suppress
occasionally	queue	susceptible
occur	quiet	tendency
occurrence	recede	tragedy
omitted	receive	twelfth
opportunity	recommend	undoubtedly
originally	referred	until
parallel	relieve	view
parliament	repetition	Wednesday
pastime	reprieve	woollen
permanent	rhythm	yield
permissible	scarcely	you're
persevere	seize	zealous
physical	sentence	

F. Spelling Errors in Transcription

It is only too easy to make spelling errors when transcribing shorthand notes. The following pairs of words are particular pitfalls, and even the most intelligent of students will choose the wrong word when intent on the shorthand. You are advised to study the list carefully and to make sure that you know the distinction between the words in each pair.

altogether	all together	hire	higher
beach	beech	in to	into
canvas	canvass	its	it's
carat	caret	later	latter
cereal	serial	lead	led

check	cheque	licence	license
chose	choose	lose	loose
company's	companies	past	passed
confident	confidant	plain	plane
council	counsel	practise	practice
correspondence	correspondents	principal	principle
cue	queue	quiet	quite
currant	current	rack	wrack
dependent	dependant	read	reed
draft	draught	session	cession
dying	dyeing	sew	sow
faint	feint	stationary	stationery
flare	flair	steel	steal
formally	formerly	to two	too
summery	summary	wet	whet
taught	taut	whether	weather
there	their	whose	who's
tire	tyre		

Be careful of the following words in transcription:

speech   pre*cede*   copy*right*   play*wright*   Brit*ain*

G. Supplementary Vocabulary and Spelling Lists

enervating	eligible	debtor	respectively
incoherent	posthumous	embargo	specification
intercede	corroborate	schedule	credentials
scrutiny	consecutive	preliminary	concession
liaison	sceptical	facilities	personnel
auxiliary	diverge	enumerate	synopsis
proficient	judicious	endorse	facsimile
superfluous	arbitration	draft	brochure
explicit	negligible	adjudicate	circular
guarantee	allude	valuation	pamphlet
ambiguous	beneficial	promulgate	inconsequential
irrational	crucial	allocation	simultaneously
supplementary	assiduous	infallible	inventory
digression	negotiate	appease	anomaly

lucrative	irresponsible	prevalent	interpolate
eventuality	disparity	peremptory	feign
apposite	intervene	accredited	aggravate
nomination	redundant	acquiesce	accentuate
constituency	extenuating	amalgamation	anticipate
controversy	concede	indemnify	transitory
imprudent	momentous	asterisk	cynical
prefatory	impetuous	deterrent	equivalent
capacity	designate	appoint	infiltrate
investigate	convention	conformity	irreparable
evasive	subordinate	colloquial	mortgage
retrograde	remittance	rejection	response
astute	arbitrary	voucher	resources
nominee	consultation	competent	competitive
alienate	statistical	substantive	influential
sponsor	exigency	prolonged	petition
inveigle	promissory	bankruptcy	mercantile
innocuous	proprietary	ancillary	executor
debenture	codicil	commendatory	sanction
inordinate	destitute	testimonial	commensurate
trenchant	culminate	liquidation	municipal
desultory	opportune	preferential	emulate
onerous	invigilate	consignment	inaugural
honorarium	integrate	fluctuate	retrospective
quandary	obligatory	aggregate	compromise
connivance	stringent	affluence	interim
commodity	indictable	subpoena	attorney
verbatim	adjournment	foreclose	litigation
leasehold	guarantor	solicitor	barrister
prospectus	stabilize	felonious	affidavit
apathetic	concurrence	conveyance	injunction
requisition	contingent	lien	surety
fraudulent	co-ordination	redress	chancery
fiscal	entail	residuary	indenture
estrangement	investment	perjury	infringement
defection	speculative	duress	statutory

coerce	refractory	incidence	exchequer
articulate	compilation	compunction	allotment
psychology	productivity	retrenchment	cumulative
cavil	actuary	impinge	endorsement
incontestable	naïve	reparation	freightage
invidious	subjective	purport	jeopardize
habitually	salvage	corollary	securities
underwrite	prolific	ulterior	inequitable
presumptive	appraisal	corporate	legislate
censure	overt	quixotic	disingenuous

H. **Abbreviations**

1. In the following exercises you are required to give the complete form for each abbreviation. Try to do this, at first without the aid of a reference book, writing down those abbreviations with which you are familiar. Then use a reference book to confirm your answers and to help you with the others.

(a) COMMERCIAL

dept	E. & O.E.	D/o	c.i.f.
Co.	b/f	O/a	a.a.r.
C.O.D.	o/a	P & L	P/A
c/o	Exs	o/d	J/A
A/C	fwd	l.s.	ex div.
A/c	Gr. Wt	c/-	f.a.q.
cr.	Inv.	r.p.	a/v
P.O.	C.B.	L/C	P.N.
R.P.	D/n	f.o.b.	B/E
mfr	D.N.	f.o.r.	B/L

(b) ORDERS, AWARDS, AND QUALIFICATIONS

The following abbreviations are used after a person's name to indicate a decoration he has been awarded, a qualification he has obtained, the award of a Royal Order, or the qualified membership of a certain society. First, make a list of the abbreviations under their appropriate headings, then give the full form of each:

B.A.	A.R.A.	B.C.L.	C.G.M.
D.F.C.	K.C.V.O.	F.R.S.L.	F.R.Z.S.
K.C.S.I.	A.C.W.A.	D.D.	B.Sc. (Eng.)
P.C.	K.G.	D.S.O.	A.M.I.Mech. E.
F.S.A.A.	T.D.	M.P.	D.B.E.
J.P.	F.R.G.S.	Ll.B.	F.R.C.S.
G.C.M.G.	Ph.D.	V.C.	Bart.
F.R.S.	Q.C.	O.B.E.	B. Mus.
K.B.E.	M.C.	F.R.I.B.A.	D. Lit.
F.C.I.S.	A.R.C.A.	A.I.I.A.	L.R.A.M.

N.B. When a person has several titles, orders, etc., they are arranged after his or her name in the following order:

1. those conferred by the Crown
2. university degrees
3. non-university qualifications

e.g.—Sir John Smith, K.C.B., M.C., Ph.D., F.R.S.

(*c*) BOOKS AND PRINTING

MS	cf.	lit.
4to	i.e.	fig.
8vo	viz.	w.f.
pp.	loc. cit.	n.p. (2)
fcp	l.c.	n.d.
ital.	tr.	
q.v.	cap (2)	
op. cit.	N.B.	
et seq.	fol.	
ibid.	ca.	

(*d*) INTERNATIONAL ORGANIZATIONS

U.N.O.	I.C.A.O.
G.A.T.T.	U.P.U.
U.N.I.C.E.F.	I.T.U.
N.A.T.O.	P.E.N.
U.N.E.S.C.O.	ECOSOC
O.E.E.C.	I.M.F.

I.L.O.	W.M.O.
I.R.O.	I.C.J.
I.T.O.	E.P.U.
W.H.O.	E.C.E.

(e) Air Transport

B.E.A.	A.I.I.
B.O.A.C.	P.A.A.
S.A.A.	P.I.A.
S.A.S.	Q.E.A.
T.C.A.	T.W.A.

(f) Armed Services

R.A.C.	R.E.M.E.
R.N.V.R.	W.R.A.F.
R.A.M.C.	W.R.N.S.
F.A.A.	R.A.S.C.
R.A.F.	R.M.

(g) National Organizations

R.S.P.C.A.	A.A.A.
P.D.S.A.	L.T.A.
N.S.P.C.C.	B.R.D.C.
W.I.	B.B.C.
W.V.S.	B.M.A.
T.U.C.	I.T.A.
F.B.I.	F.A.
S.P.C.K.	Y.H.A.
Y.M.C.A.	A.A.
C.O.I.	N.C.B.

(h) Trades Unions, etc.

E.T.U.	N.F.U.
N.A.L.G.O.	A.E.U.
N.U.T.	T. & G.W.U.
N.U.R.	C.S.C.A.
N.U.J.	N.U.M.

(*i*) MISCELLANEOUS

B.M.	M.
O.E.D.	c.c.
S.R. & O.	b.h.p.
C.I.D.	m.p.g.
M.C.C.	D.N.B.
B.U.P.	Q.E.D.
B.P. (2)	M.F.H.
P.L.A.	R.S.V.P.
D.V.	P.T.O.
T.T.	A.D.
E.P.T.	M & B
P.A.Y.E.	I.C.I.
A.P.	B.I.F.
R.N.L.I.	B.T.U.
R.D.C.	G.P.
R.I.P.	G.M.T.
H.R.H.	B.R.
V.I.P.	I.W.
A.S.L.I.B.	B.R.M.
L.P.T.B.	B.S.A.

2. *General Exercises*

(*a*) Explain the abbreviations in each of the following:

   (i) Col. P. E. Hume, C.B.E., D.S.O., M.C.
   (ii) J. R. Smith, M.Sc.(Econ.), B.Com., Ll.B.
  (iii) R. A. Jones, M.D., F.R.C.P.
  (iv) Sir Norman Brown, K.B.E., C.B., D.Sc.
   (v) Arthur Bright, M.A., B.Mus., F.R.C.O.
  (vi) P. R. Kirk, M.I.Prod.E., A.M.I.Mech.E., A.M.I.I.A.
 (vii) L. J. Price, M.Sc., F.G.S., A.M.Inst.Pet.
(viii) B. M. Maws, B.Sc.(Eng.), A.C.G.I., D.I.C.
  (ix) A. M. Sutter, D.Sc., F.R.I.C., F.I.M.
   (x) Sir William Cox, K.B.E., C.M.G., D.F.C., F.R.C.P.

(*b*) What do the following notes and footnotes mean?

    (i) For further information cf. Jones—"Brit. Con." cap. V para. 7 *et seq.*

    (ii) [1] *ibid.* vol. ii cap. 4 pp. 132–135.

    (iii) (*vide* Gretton, *Antiquities of Lower Mesopotamia* (Camb. Mass.) 1929, ii, V, 32–38).

    (iv) Smith *v.* Granger (1892) 2 QB. 384.

    (v) *Op. cit.* p. 145 and p. 179. & *passim.*

    (vi) Companies Act, 1929, (19 and 20 Geo. 5, c. 23).

    (vii) GROC/CONF/TOB., Honiton. Av.t.o. £150 p.w. Long lse. av. Flat accom. £1,750, s.a.v. BOX 438, Daily News.

    (viii) Cf. -ing, -ed *supra.*

    (ix) [3] *Journal of Psychology* cxii, 143–9 *q.v.*

    (x) James, A. R. "New Developments in Ethnology" (Proc. of Antiqu. Soc., N.S., vol. ix, Camb. 1894, pp. 36–49).

I. Foreign Words and Phrases

The use of foreign words and phrases in everyday speech and writing is regarded as a mark of affectation, especially when such hackneyed phrases are used as:

Latin	*French*
ab initio	amour propre
in extenso	nouveau riche
de novo	au fait
in toto	raison d'être

Many such expressions can be adequately conveyed in our own language. Why say that something is *à la mode* when we can say that it is fashionable? Use it by all means for particular dishes—bœuf a là mode—but be careful about the special meaning! The occupants of an aircraft may be relieved to touch down on *terra firma*, but why not say "dry land," or merely say that they are "pleased to land"?

Avoid such word snobbery, but also realize that many foreign words have become a part of our language, some now unrecognizable as aliens. The test is whether an imported word expresses a shade of meaning for which there is no real English equivalent. Words such as ennui, post mortem, chic, blasé, précis, menu, etcetera, give useful service and are therefore acceptable.

Foreign words and phrases have become part of technical and commercial vocabulary, and you should be aware of the use and meaning of certain of these phrases. Terms such as *dementia praecox*, in psychiatry; *reductio ad absurdum*, in logic; *chiaroscuro*, in painting; *conservatoire*, in music; are specialized terms which do not concern us here, but there are many Latin and French words and phrases which have become a normal feature of legal, commercial, and administrative vocabulary. In the following exercises a selection of these is given; the meanings are arranged in the opposite column but in a jumbled sequence. Rearrange the meanings against the expressions they represent and show in sentences how each foreign expression is used.

Jumbled Meanings

1. ad valorem
   - bona fides
   - pro rata
   - per contra
   - quid pro quo
   - pro forma
   - ultra vires
   - stet
   - sine qua non
   - non sequitur

   on the opposite side
   compensation
   contradictory result
   indispensable condition
   for the sake of form
   honest intention
   let it stand
   in proportion to value
   beyond the powers
   proportionally

2. sine die
   - sub judice
   - in camera
   - onus probandi
   - sub rosa
   - prima facie
   - flagrante delicto
   - status quo
   - nolle prosequi
   - inter alia

   in confidence
   in the act of offending
   unchanged position
   stay of proceedings
   not yet decided
   among other things
   not in open court
   burden of proof
   from the first impression
   indefinitely adjourned

3. ad hoc   incidental remark
   ex officio   intrinsically
   obiter dictum   deputy
   persona grata   in place of a parent
   mutatis mutandis   for the special purpose
   per se   in every part
   locum tenens   acceptable person
   in loco parentis   in virtue of one's office
   passim   authoritative
   ex cathedra   with necessary alteration of details

4. carte blanche   department where letters await
   vis-à-vis   full powers   [personal collection
   laissez-faire   ambiguous expression
   poste-restante   sensational law suit
   force majeure   no govt. interference
   cause célèbre   opposite to
   amour propre   violent change of government
   double entendre   personal pride
   coup d'état   done and no longer worth arguing
   fait accompli   irresistible compulsion

5. agent provocateur   habitual visitor
   cadre   officer carrying orders
   habitué   feat of strength
   aide-de-camp   framework
   communiqué   private conversation
   tour de force   weary of pleasure
   dossier   official disclosure
   tête-à-tête   controller of a commercial venture
   blasé   personal record
   entrepreneur   person who detects offenders by
                                 tempting them to wrong action

SECTION II

SPEED AND ACCURACY EXERCISES

The following section contains a series of exercises designed to test rapid application of a knowledge of English. The exercises should be given regularly and a time-limit set for completion depending upon the attainment and ability of the group.

The pattern of each exercise is as follows:

1. Spelling
2. Word division
3. Vocabulary
4. Vocabulary
5. Grammar
6. Grammar
7. Punctuation
8. Sentence Correction
9. Idiom
10. General.

Although preliminary study and knowledge is presumed, points of revision are given in the Appendices.

A

1. Complete the spelling of the following words with *ei* or *ie*:

dec–tful	for–gn	rec–ve
s–ze	s–ge	h–ght
ch–f	fr–nd	n–ther
ach–ve		

2. Divide each of the following words, where necessary, for a line-end division:

continuous	frustrate	carefully	absolutely
until	entertain	running	arrangement
influential	eccentricity		

3. Give suitable synonyms for each of the following words:

despair	aggravate	eliminate	impose
odd	animated	antique	staid
endeavour	overbearing		

4. Show the distinction between the words in each of the following pairs by using in explanatory sentences:

principal/principle   continual/continuous
dependent/dependant

5. Add the suffix -*able* to each of the following words:

move	manage	desire	peace	note
change	mistake	service	advise	forgive

6. Use each of the words given below in a sentence to indicate the preposition(s) that should normally follow it:

entrust   beware   inveigle   exempt   deter

7. Insert commas where necessary in the following sentences:

(a) "You are sir a cold calculating brutal person."
(b) Perhaps the quickest way and certainly the easiest will be to send the goods by rail.
(c) The goods having arrived the sales department became busy.
(d) The person who made this should be ashamed of himself.
(e) The last item which was not really important was deferred until the next meeting.

8. Rewrite these sentences correctly:

(a) He is always better at cricket than me.
(b) He is more successful at portraits than any living painter.
(c) Every one must continue to play their part.
(d) Having displayed the goods in a prominent position the new line in soap powder sold quickly.
(e) The proposal was put forward to earnestly study the new constitution.

9. Compose sentences to show clearly the meanings of the following idiomatic phrases:

not a leg to stand on
above board
fight shy
come down to earth
put the cart before the horse

10. Convert the following into Roman numerals:

44   52   99   176   200

B

1. Rewrite the following passage putting the correct letters into the incomplete words:

> Th–r eyes were on the game, the ha–a–ing battle being fought on –ncred–bly –nequal terms between t– teams sk–ly selected for –ndur–nce, p–sev–r–nce, and experience, but with one side po–s–ing an awkward and un–th–x style of play.

2. Divide each of the following words, where necessary, for a line-end division:

secretary	commonplace	plausible	essential
whether	distressing	Aberdeen	understand
possibility	sensitive		

3. Distinguish between words in each of the pairs by using in sentences:

affect/effect   precipitate/precipitous
transitive/transitory

4. Give simpler versions for these formal words:

accommodate	donation	peruse	cease
commence	complete (*adj.*)	evince	sustain
expedite	purchase		

5. Complete this table:

	Past Simple Tense	Past Participle
Wake	....	waked
Waken	....	....
Awake	awoke	....
Awaken	....	awakened

6. Add a suffix containing *ion* to each of the following roots:

amputa–	sensa–	deci–	cessa–
legisla–	acquisi–	televi–	remi–
admi–	sedi–		

B

7. Insert apostrophes where required in these phrases:

S† Jamess Square.	Childrens games.
Its effect wont last.	Mens shoes repaired.
For goodness sake dont cry.	Mind your ps and qs.
Theres a years work here.	Ill answer the phone.
My answers right, yours wrong.	Theyre over the hill.

8. Rewrite these sentences correctly:

(a) The collection of string, paper, cardboard, and books were passed to the packing department.

(b) That is the person whom I think is the new prefect.

(c) He could either spend the day swimming or sailing.

(d) He needs his suit pressed badly.

(e) He would not tolerate me playing the trombone.

9. Use the following words in sentences to indicate the correct prepositions required after them:

compensate   affinity   differ   commiserate
abstain

10. Convert the following passage into direct speech, beginning, "The inspector asked . . ."

The inspector was anxious to discover why Mr Brown had been found in possession of the stolen money, but Mr Brown was unable to explain. He produced the excuse that he had left his case in the shop and had not touched it until the day of the robbery. It was then that the money had been found. The inspector was suddenly suspicious, and asked why Mr Brown had not touched the case for several days. Mr Brown gave the simple excuse that he had been absent from his job with a cold.

C

1. Complete the spelling of these words:

a–ress	arg–ment	spe–ch	ab–en–e	f–rty
Wed–day	m–rm–r	begi–ing	amat–r	ei–th

2. Divide as for line-end division:

catalogue	overwhelm	substantial	committee
decision	invidious	absolutely	fortune
comprehend	detention		

3. Distinguish between the words in each of the following pairs by using them in a sentence:

authentic/genuine dilemma/difficulty
invent/discover

4. Give a one-word equivalent for each of the following short definitions:

(a) able to speak two languages equally well *bilingual*
(b) a person who hates mankind
(c) squeamish and hard to please *+ artibes*
(d) severely simple *austere*
(e) not spontaneous, but following tradition *conventional*

5. Give the past participles of these verbs:

lie (2)	lay	speak	drink	see
arise	write	swim	flow	fly

6. Rearrange the words in the right-hand column so that each is against the word of which it is a synonym:

vague	inference
deceived	thoughtful
implication	valuation
pensive	unconnected
estimation	duped

7. Punctuate these sentences:

(a) The man shouted stop at once he said
(b) Did you know asked Jim that the new edition of the encyclopaedia is now available
(c) Theres no doubt at all said the lecturer that some scientists efforts will have far reaching results
(d) I considered that Smith who knew only part of the way would prove an unreliable guide
(e) Stop shouted the guard stop no further theres danger ahead

8. Correct the following sentences:

(a) He is one of those cricketers who always plays a sound innings.
(b) The managing director reported that the machinery will be delivered later in the week.
(c) He presented an illuminated address to Mr Smith and a cheque.

(*d*) John always prefers to go by coach rather than by car.
(*e*) The road to the south is more smoother than the north.

9. Rewrite the following sentences inserting the correct prepositions:

(*a*) He affixed a stamp —— the envelope before putting the letter —— the post box.
(*b*) He is averse —— playing tennis, but is quite adept —— cricket.
(*c*) Although the river abounded —— fish, the angler was unable to succeed —— his efforts.
(*d*) Compared —— his brother he is a quiet boy, but his manners are in distinct contrast —— his appearance.
(*e*) He gazed —— the window at the river, thinking of the time he sailed —— the Thames from Greenwich to Kingston.

10. Convert the following Roman numerals:

XXXIV   LVIII   XLIII   LXXIX   XCIX

D

1. Add the appropriate suffix -*able* or -*ible* to the following roots:

access–   amen–   poss–   defens–   cap–
regrett–   divis–   intellig–   despic–   permiss–

2. Divide the following words for line-end:

understand   successful   mixture   possible
something   constantly   replacement
vivacious   insidious   infiltrate

3. Distinguish between the words in each of the following pairs by using in sentences:

staid/stayed   flare/flair
plain/plane   throes/throws

4. For each of the following short definitions provide one word ending in -*ate*:

(*a*) A person who pleads on behalf of some one in public.
(*b*) Insist upon something as the essential part of an agreement.
(*c*) Express disapproval of an action.
(*d*) Place apart or alone.
(*e*) Express the sense of a passage in another language.

5. Form adjectives (other than participle equivalents) from the following nouns and verbs:

wool	apply	cause	pity	quality
analysis	candour	commend	satisfy	consider

6. Indicate the prepositions that normally follow these words:

contrast (*as a verb*)	essential	instil
indifferent	independent	

7. Punctuate and paragraph the following:

The manager searched his desk where are my papers miss todd they should be where you put them but theyre not then mr smith they must have been filed why filed when i had clearly marked them for immediate action im sorry mr smith i will find them for you immediately

8. Correct the following sentences:

(*a*) Every one of the guests have their own plates.
(*b*) He is unable to play cricket like other boys.
(*c*) It is precisely those sort of actions that arouse ill-feeling.
(*d*) We know the newspapers obtained one of those two interviews, but we are glad it is the most factual.
(*e*) I am not certain who the books was given to.

9. Express a metaphorical sense of each of these words by using it in a sentence:

cut	deep	road	steep	veil

10. Compose a short paragraph containing the following words and showing clearly their meaning and interrelation:

accounts	deficit	ledger	balance
creditor	trade		

E

1. Add suffixes containing *ion* to the following part words:

specializa–	deriva–	demarca–	dicta–
ammuni–	permi–	divi–	provi–
acclama–	embarka–		

2. Give three rules—and examples—for division of words at line-end.

3. Distinguish between the words in each of the following pairs by using in sentences:

company's/companies   compare/compère
brooch/broach   treaties/treatise

4. Provide suitable antonyms for the following words:

abrupt   reality   luxury   enmity   accelerate
destroy   import   argue   sever   relaxed

5. Write sentences to show the difference in the use of *shall* and *will*, *may* and *can*.

6. Give five examples of words ending in the suffix *-ible*, and five ending in the suffix *-able*.

7. Insert commas where necessary in the following sentences:

(*a*) Below further information is given of men who are qualified to take the course.

(*b*) Being unsafe the old dark house which was no longer occupied stood lonely and eerie.

(*c*) It is a pleasure my friend to be visiting your locality but I am afraid that I cannot stay long.

8. Explain and correct the ambiguity in the following sentences:

(*a*) You are the last person I want to see.

(*b*) No one has been in the office for a week.

(*c*) Before the Indians could attack the emigrants they were all killed.

9. The following words have a correct use but are often used in a 'loose' way. Write sentences to show the difference between these two uses of each word:

aggravate   nice   rotten   dreadful

10. Rewrite the following collection of short sentences as one *multiple* sentence:

Dorothy is usually a good tennis player. This week, however, her game has been very ragged. She has played several good strokes. Her base line returns go too often into the net. It seems that she is overtired. That often has an adverse effect on a player.

F

1. Complete the spelling of the following words:

prof–sion   suc–sion   end–v–r   cel–oid
pr–v–l–ge   rep–tit–on   temp–r–ry   d–l–p–d–tion
perm–s–ble   comp–r–t–ve

2. Suitably divide, for line-end, the following words:

forgetting   important   grateful   presidential
transport   observant   unanimous   audience
refrigerate   occupation

3. Give simpler one-word equivalents of the following formal words:

emoluments   veritable   imbibe   malefactor
imperceptible spurious   grandiose   corporate
parsimonious   prevaricate

4. Show the distinction between the words in each of these pairs by using them in sentences:

contort/distort   horde/hoard
physical/psychical

5. Give the plurals of the following:

man-servant   passer-by   Miss Smith   spoonful
trade union

6. Explain the significance of the following prefixes and give an example of the use of each:

pre-   circum-   bi-   sub-   trans-

7. Punctuate each of the following sentences in two ways to show differences in meaning:

(a) The Inspector said the teacher was incompetent.
(b) That was the person he noticed standing near the kiosk.
(c) There was a fierce argument and at the end I left him fuming and angry.
(d) The English who are uninformed know nothing of Continental politics.

8. Convert these examples of commercial jargon into good English:

(a) We are wholly at a loss to understand.
(b) It is felt to be necessary.
(c) We will immediately despatch.
(d) We have instituted the necessary enquiries.
(e) We shall take a very early opportunity of writing.

9. Write sentences to illustrate the difference made by the prepositions in each of the following pairs:

responsible for	responsible to
differ from	differ with
correspond with	correspond to

10. Construct a full dictionary definition for *one* of the following (derivation where possible):

chauffeur   omnibus   telephone

G

1. Give three spelling rules and an example of each.
2. Divide the following words as for a line-end division:

audibility	commensurate	circumference
acknowledge	deciduous	overseer
furniture	obligations	advertisement
exercises		

3. Distinguish between the words in each of these pairs by using them in suitable explanatory sentences:

complement/compliment	council/counsel
session/cession	enquire/inquire

4. For each of the following definitions provide one word ending in -*ance*:

(a) Overbearing and haughty behaviour.
(b) The carrying out of a theatrical event or public exhibition.
(c) An action or object annoying or injurious to other people.
(d) Moderation in speech, eating, or drinking.
(e) Practice of enduring and permitting social actions with which one does not necessarily agree.

5. Give the past participles of these verbs:

<blockquote>

sit   sweep   spoil   spell   spin

</blockquote>

6. Form adjectives from these words:

<blockquote>

grain   theory   insist   care   discretion
example   wear   fraction custom attend

</blockquote>

7. Write sentences to show the use of each of the following marks of punctuation:

    (a) dash
    (b) hyphen
    (c) quotation marks in measurements
    (d) apostrophe to show certain plurals
    (e) parentheses to show references

8. Correct the following sentences:

  (a) He has a white elephant in his commercial greenhouse.
  (b) They wanted him for a midweek match but he could only play cricket of a Sunday.
  (c) He was no sooner in bed when he fell in a deep sleep.
  (d) He stopped at the tobacco kiosk which made him lose his train.
  (e) He told his team that each of them will be able to reach the ground by oneself.

9. Use the following idiomatic phrases in sentences to show their meaning:

<blockquote>

free lance   a bottle-neck   a clean sweep
cut and dried   lose face

</blockquote>

10. Give the Roman numerals for the following:

<blockquote>

1177   1066   1473   1500   1933

</blockquote>

H

1. Complete the part words in this passage, spelling them correctly:

I should like a s–p–r–te a–reement drawn up, especia–y in v–w of the dis–pointing way in which the la–ers dealt with that par–el case which I saw refe–d to in the local press. However regre–able it may be to rec–ve this advi–e, please regard it as me–ly a precautionary measure.

2. Divide these words, where necessary, as for line-end division:

shipping	nationality	complacent	children
souvenir	also	monument	gather
Manchester	receiving		

3. Give a synonym for each of the following words:

spacious	requisition	official	ultimate
jocular	gratify	encourage	disturb
changeable	deceitful		

4. For each of the italicized phrases use a one word equivalent:

(a) The meaning of the word was not clear from *the parts preceding and following it.*

(b) Because he was *unable to read or write* a great many opportunities were closed to him.

(c) The witness was guilty of *swearing to a statement she knew to be false.*

(d) The furniture was shabby and needed *restoring to its previous good condition.*

(e) He always had a worried look and appeared never to *adopt a less tense manner.*

5. Give the comparative and superlative of the following adjectives and adverbs:

likely	shy	often	bad	much
aware	noble	wisely	little	terrible

6. Select the gerunds and present participles in the following passage and arrange them in two appropriately headed columns:

Watching the darting movements of the birds was an engrossing pastime. Their fluttering in the nearby trees was accompanied by a raucous chattering followed by a sudden burst of squawking. Several birds, forsaking the trees, began circling above his hiding-place seeming suddenly to sense his presence.

7. Insert hyphens where necessary in the following:

running water	home made	witness box
single seater	full stop	

8. Correct these sentences:

(*a*) I will be glad to see you to-morrow if you could manage to come.

(*b*) Neither of the two speakers who visited our meeting were very impressive.

(*c*) Having repaired his bicycle it now runs smoothly.

(*d*) Why do they insist on me playing the piano?

(*e*) This is the finest built of any concert hall.

9. Give an example of each of the following figures of speech:

metaphor   antithesis   irony

pun   personification

10. Rewrite this abbreviated passage in full:

W rfce to yr ltr o t 15 Mar abt t mtg tt shd h bn held this aftn, I must tell y tt t nbr o people in attdce ws so small tt t bd immdly gave its opn tt anr mtg shd b held at abt 4 ock next Fri aftn.

I

1. Complete the following words:

inc–h–r–n–y   c–met–ry   c–t–l–gue

ac–l–r–t–r   gr–m–one   hum–r–s

ac–m–late   F–r–nh–t   c–rp–r–tion

p–rm–n–nt

2. Give five different examples of instances in which you would *not* divide a word at line-end.

3. Give a single word—a verb ending in *-ate*—for each of these short definitions:

(*a*) make something more difficult

(*b*) introduce something novel

(*c*) confirm a statement by giving evidence

(*d*) decide upon a case or claim

(*e*) bring back to life

4. What is the significance of the suffix *-logy* in the following words? Give the meaning of each word.

biology   anthropology   sociology   zoology

geology   entomology   ethnology   etymology

pathology   theology

5. Write sentences illustrating the use of:

(a) an absolute phrase
(b) an infinitive phrase as subject
(c) a participle phrase
(d) gerund phrase as object
(e) prepositional phrase

6. Give the plurals of these 'borrowed' foreign words:

index (2)   formula (2)   axis   radius   addendum

7. Draw the outline of an envelope and write or type in it the following address:

wate and ramchurch ltd educational supplies cartographic department 53 st swithins square london s w 3

8. Correct the following sentences:

(a) Each of the men who was taking part in the job were fully trained.
(b) He wished to have spoken to you over the phone yesterday.
(c) Sitting in the front row the screen looked distorted.
(d) He looked for the time at his watch which reminded him of his appointment.
(e) News were scarce. The people had not been told hardly anything.

9. Explain the meanings of the following proverbial sayings:

A nod is as good as a wink to a blind horse.
An ounce of favour is worth more than a pound of justice.
The road to hell is paved with good intentions.

10. Write sentences to show the difference between a defining and a non-defining relative clause.

J

1. Complete the spelling of the following words:

a–reviate   ac–m–date   rec–mend   embar–sing
ex–r–ise   priv–l–ge   advis–ble   cat–g–ry
rep–tation   med–c–ne

2. Divide the following words, where necessary, as if for line-ending:

petroleum	obnoxious	amplify	noticeable
implications	candidate	always	regretting
beneath	nothing		

3. Give one word for each of these definitions:

(a) avoidance of work by feigning illness
(b) unable to pay debts
(c) speak without notes or preparation
(d) stage of recovery after an illness
(e) value too highly

4. Arrange the following adverbs in order of strength, the strongest one last:

madly, quickly, rapidly, swiftly, hurriedly, precipitately, frenziedly, feverishly.

5. Give the plurals of these words:

crisis   syllabus   series   criterion   analysis

6. Rewrite the following sentences, choosing the correct word from each pair in parentheses:

(a) He placed the tools (altogether/all together) in one case.
(b) He carried out the task so successfully that he felt quite (complacent/complaisant) about it.
(c) After the party, the guests began to feel the (affects/effects) of over-eating.
(d) The conjurer waved his wand, opened the box to reveal its emptiness, and the (illusion/delusion) was complete.
(e) He washed, dressed, and went (into/in to) dinner.

7. Insert the necessary commas in the following sentences:

(a) Care consideration and helpful advice are required.
(b) The 42000 men who were required for the army's offensive were not available but further reserves although of inferior fighting qualities were obtained from another theatre of war.
(c) The men having finished the job the foreman sent them home.
(d) As regards the holidays many if not most of the party will take the shorter route.
(e) "John please close the door even if you are going out again and do not forget to put the mat back."

8. Explain and correct the ambiguity in these sentences:

(a) They were alone together. Two pairs of eyes met and they talked of this and that, their shyness gone.
(b) They drank beer drawn from the wood which was very tasty.
(c) She played tunes for her friends on the piano.

9. Give a figurative use of each of these geographical terms:

strata   oasis   climate   latitude   summit

10. Arrange in proper sequence the qualifications, etc., which follow these names:

Major General Sir John Smith,	F.R.C.O., Bart., M.C., M.A.
Jonathan Green Esq.,	A.M.I.C.E., C.G.M., B.Sc., T.D.

K

1. Rewrite the following passage, correctly spelling the incomplete words:

There has been a def–n–te increase in errors of gramm–r. I have been embar–s–ed to find that I have rec–ved several sep–r–te answers with similar un–c–sary mistakes. These should not oc–r and there must be more practi–e and less wo–ly thought.

2. Divide the following words, where necessary, as for line-ending:

smattering	ignoramus	technical	commercial
rehabilitate	organization	delegate	denied
ambiguous	overwhelm		

3. Rewrite the following sentences inserting the correct word, from the pair in parentheses, in the blank space:

(a) The student had written an —— sentence and the lecturer found its meaning ——. (*uncertain/ambiguous*)
(b) The detectives managed to —— from the population information about the —— still. (*illicit/elicit*)
(c) He was feeling unwell and a drop of the necessary —— provided him with a suitable —— to carry on. (*stimulus/stimulant*)
(d) It was a —— fact that the —— odour could be smelt across a wide area. (*distinct/distinctive*)

(*e*) She was —— pretty, but —— fond of parties and fast cars. (*excessively/exceedingly*)

4. Give one word for each of the following short definitions:

(*a*) form giving particulars of goods sold
(*b*) note sent to remind some one of money due and setting out the transactions
(*c*) an informal letter without a signature
(*d*) a notice printed for sending round to several people
(*e*) a brief summary of the proceedings of a meeting

5. Form adjectives (*not* participles) from the following:

star	co-operate	anxiety	symptom	praise
diagnosis	advise	imply	divide	anticipate

6. Rewrite the following words showing whether they should be a single word, hyphenated, or separate words:

make believe	head master	every where
school boy	old fashioned	mantel piece
eye witness	to morrow	note book
night watch man		

7. Explain three uses of the dash and give an example of each.

8. Correct the following sentences:

(*a*) Each of the workmen are so careless that they must accept responsibility for any accident.
(*b*) He ought never to have drank that tinted water until it had been stereotyped.
(*c*) Neither the wish to eagerly engage the enemy or the desire to achieve fame was present in the mind of the little private.
(*d*) Negotiations having broken down they returned to their hotels.
(*e*) It is a coincidence that yours and my birthdays are on the same day.

9. Use the following idiomatic phrases in sentences to show clearly their meaning:

null and void	at a premium
to cut one's losses	part and parcel
to split hairs	

10. Convert the following passage into direct speech:

The chairman said that the previous meeting had been too prolonged and expressed the wish that there should not be a repetition of the delaying tactics which certain members had used. He was determined to keep to the agenda. Several members were annoyed. Mr Smith expressed his regret that the chairman's comment had been so brusque. It was in some ways an unnecessary slight upon the members' characters. The chairman interrupted to say that such a slight had not been intended.

L

1. Give an example of each of the following:

    (a) a word with a silent *g*
    (b) a word with a diphthong
    (c) a word of four syllables
    (d) a word of three syllables with both prefix and suffix
    (e) a word with a silent *ch*

2. Divide the following words, where necessary, as for line-ending:

sentence	Jenkins	beginning	activity
heather	profession	brevity	acknowledge
arrogance	sententious		

3. Rewrite the following sentences choosing the correct word from those in parentheses:

    (a) They could not tolerate the new manager because he was overbearing and (official/officiate/officious).
    (b) I cannot agree with him because he holds opinions (averse/adverse) to my own.
    (c) After his downfall the dictator took to drink, lived in filth and poverty, and became a most (contemptuous/contemptible) person.
    (d) Although education is almost a public utility, parties in the House tend to make it a (political/politic) issue.
    (e) The new dramatist has a most (imaginative/imaginary) way of treating his theme.

4. Give an adjective for each of the following short definitions:

cannot be ended	leading to a decision
made easy	cannot be regained
easily read	

5. Show, by using them in sentences, how each of the following words may be used as the different parts of speech indicated:

round	noun, verb, preposition
still	adjective, noun, adverb
near	adjective, adverb, preposition

6. Form abstract nouns from the following words:

deep	sensitive	provocative	exceed	amiable
capable	friendly	friend	blue	curve

7. Give an example of each of the following:

(a) a number of four figures occurring without the comma
(b) two different uses of the question mark
(c) the use of dashes for parenthesis
(d) the use of the apostrophe to show possession
(e) the use of parentheses to provide a reference within a sentence

8. Correct the redundancy in the following sentences:

(a) He has returned back to the office again after his illness.
(b) The stupefied crowd gazed in amazement at the strange phenomenon.
(c) There is one undeniable fact, which you cannot argue against—the cost of living has undoubtedly gone up.
(d) One of my favourite games, which I like very much, is tennis.
(e) I can send only five pounds in repayment of that debt of money I owe you.

9. Insert the correct prepositions in the blank spaces:

(a) The construction firm entered —— an agreement with the sub-contractors.
(b) At the end of the day he entered —— the ledger.
(c) He soon entered —— the spirit of the discussion.
(d) The question of failure did not enter —— their considerations.
(e) He entered —— the subject with some hesitancy.

10. Convert the following Roman numerals:

MCML	MDCCXXXVIII
MCXL	CDV
MCLVIII	

M

1. Complete the spelling of these words:

ign–r–nce	hyg–ne	bel–v–ble	inno–en–e
man–vre	enc–cl–p–d–	d–struct–ble	
cat–g–ry	ex–il–rate	el–g–b–lity	

2. Divide the following words, where necessary, as for line-ending:

plausibility	translucent	subtlety	volunteer
whimsical	veracious	worshipped	quarrelling
millimetre	monosyllabic		

3. Arrange these words in order, ending with the one which has the strongest meaning:

obtuse, shallow, unintellectual, frivolous, stupid, unintelligent, dull, moronic, imbecile, witless.

4. Compose a short paragraph introducing the following words to show clearly their interrelation:

efficiency	accuracy	concentration
conscientious	aptitude	

5. Form verbs from the following words:

standard	sculpture	antagonist	clarity
description	peace	little	division
fort	habitation		

6. Complete the following table of words:

length	lengthen	long	height	——	——
——	——	deep	——	practise	——
prophecy	——	——	peace	——	——

7. Punctuate the following:

please take a letter began the manager one moment mr smith while i sharpen my pencil sharpen your pencil miss green you should have done that before you came in im sorry sir you should be careful not sorry be quick there was a short delay are you ready now good then begin dear sir in reply to drat that phone.

8. Correct the following sentences:

(*a*) He found the man drinking tea reclining in an old chair.

(*b*) It was clearly a bad arrangement not only in the case of the seller but also the buyer.

(*c*) It was a very unique opportunity that was offered in the newspaper announcement.

(*d*) I am going to give you a piece of advice which I hope you will understand what I mean.

(*e*) I was rather concerned about him failing than her succeeding in the examination.

9. Use the following idiomatic phrases in sentences to show their meaning:

crocodile tears	the yellow press
an act of God	red tape
busman's holiday	

10. Draft a formal invitation to be printed and sent out on the occasion of your coming-of-age party.

N

1. Rewrite the following passage completing the spelling of the part words:

In the co–se of his in–g–ral sp–ch the Chairman refe–d to par–l–l develo–ments in other industries, some easy to g–ge others difficult to as–s because they had not been publi–i–ed.

2. Divide the following words, where necessary, as if for line-ending:

cumulative	connoisseur	convertible	blameable
riveted	diagrammatic	exercise	permissible
dissolution	eccentric		

3. Use the following words in sentences to show clearly their meaning:

cynical   subsequent   exigency   coherent   anomaly

4. For each of these verbs plus preposition write a single word suggesting the same meaning:

come upon	fall behind	give in	look for
put forward	take after	bear out	throw away
stand down	make out		

5. Complete the following table. Do not use participles:

	continue	
		abstemious
provocation		
abundance		
	impel	

6. Show, by means of a mark, where the accent falls in these words:

vicissitude	ludicrous	controversy	temporary
irreparable	presidential	metallurgy	inventory
formidable	dependent		

7. Explain four uses of the comma and give one example of each.

8. Rewrite the following passage correcting errors of grammar and style:

Correct the following sentences as quick as you can for each of the various errors are fairly easy when you know how. Being quick on the uptake unrelated participles are easy to be identified. but it is better to be on the watch for the subtle errors rather than to either concentrate on the blaring errors or to abandon the whole project.

9. Show, by using them in sentences, the difference between

write up	and	*write down*
end with	and	*end in*
submit to	and	*submit for*

10. Explain the following terms:

paraphrase	malapropism
parody	errata
footnote	

O

1. Complete the words:

transp–r–nt	s–p–r–te	ac–m–d–te	misch–v–s
j–p–rdy	extr–v–g–nce	pr–v–l–nt	p–rs–t
c–rc–mf–r–nce	ga–ty		

2. Give two examples of each of these types of word division:

    (*a*) after a prefix
    (*b*) between two consonants
    (*c*) before a suffix
    (*d*) before -*ing*
    (*e*) between two vowels

3. Give a single word for each of these short definitions:

    (*a*) not having made a will
    (*b*) unable to pay debts
    (*c*) giving of false evidence in a court
    (*d*) profitable office without work involved
    (*e*) secure against loss

4. Use the following words in sentences to show clearly their meaning:

    correlation   dispersal   installation   officious
    arduous

5. Rewrite the following short passage inserting correctly *was* or *were* in the spaces:

    Because there ⸺ a number of books missing from the office, the board ⸺ summoned to an extraordinary meeting where the news ⸺ given and each of the members ⸺ told to look for the lost books. Not one of the office clerks ⸺ to blame, neither ⸺ the cleaning staff under suspicion.

6. Give the two plural forms for each of the following words and explain the difference in meaning:

    penny   index   brother   staff

7. Demonstrate, in sentences, each of these uses of the comma:

    (*a*) to separate adjectives preceding and qualifying a noun
    (*b*) after an absolute phrase
    (*c*) to mark a non-defining relative clause
    (*d*) with a nominative of address
    (*e*) to separate a series of phrases

8. Correct these sentences:

    (*a*) If one intends to travel abroad or to occasionally pay visits to outlying parts he should be carefully prepared.

(b) "Please await until the bus stops."

(c) He gave us no idea that he will be playing the following week.

(d) It is necessary that frequent changes are made in the daily routine.

(e) Men's strength is greater than women.

9. Write sentences using these words in a metaphorical sense:

       burn   feed   sift   seize   engrave

10. Show by examples the difference between a *loose* and a *periodic* sentence.

SECTION III

LETTER-WRITING

Diagram. THE FRAMEWORK OF A BUSINESS LETTER
- A. THE LAY-OUT OF THE LETTER
- B. TYPES OF BUSINESS LETTER
- C. TONE
- D. COMMERCIAL JARGON
- E. CONVERTING COMMERCIAL JARGON
- F. EXERCISES IN THE ARRANGEMENT AND PUNCTUATION OF LETTERS
- G. RE-PHRASING AND RE-CASTING LETTERS
- H. COMPOSING LETTERS OF REPLY FROM NOTES
- I. ADDITIONAL LETTER-WRITING EXERCISES
- J. COMPOSITION OF A SERIES OF LETTERS

The Framework of a Business Letter

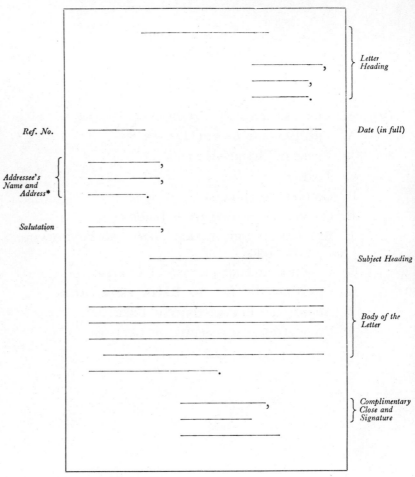

* Also known as *Inside Address*

N.B. It is important that a letter should create a good impression by being neatly set on the page, carefully typed, and properly punctuated. It is usual to type the letter in single spacing with a line space between paragraphs.

A. **The Lay-out of the Letter**

The letter framework shown in the diagram is the form generally used, but there are variations in detail according to the accepted practice of individual firms. The newly-appointed secretary or shorthand typist will be told of the company's method of letter-writing and display; in fact, many organizations have specially-prepared booklets dealing with the subject.

At this stage, however, you must follow carefully the instructions given by your typewriting lecturer for letter display.

The purpose of a neatly arranged and typed letter is to create a favourable first impression. One large firm tells its employees that every letter from the organization is a letter of goodwill, and that is no idle statement. The neat appearance of the type is important and balanced paragraphing gives a pleasing effect. Remember, too, that a short, single-spaced letter on octavo paper has a better appearance than double spacing on quarto.

The Letter Heading

This is usually printed, with the name of the firm centred at the top of the paper, and its address shown in the usual position at the right-hand side. There are, however, variations to allow for printing other information such as: telephone number, telegraphic address, other departments or factories, names of principals and directors, etc. The following letter head is a fairly typical example:

SMITH & JONES LTD

Telephone: **Motor Engineers**   48–50 HIGH STREET,
   MELSHAM 42   MELSHAM,

Managing Director: HERTS.
   A. A. SMITH

The Date

This is typed at the right-hand side of the letter, double-spaced below the address. The date should be in full, usually in the order: day, month, year. There is no need for a comma after the day, but there must be one after the month—*e.g.,*

14th December, 1957

A full stop after the year is optional, but it is the modern tendency to omit it.

Reference

Reference letters or numbers are sometimes given at the left, on the same line as the date. In simple form they may consist of the initials of the person dictating followed by the initials of the shorthand typist. Sometimes a file number is added— *e.g.*,

Our Ref: PJ/KS/373

Other references may be to file numbers, or to a client's account number. In all cases they should be quoted when replying to the letter—*e.g.*,

Our Ref: PJ/KS
Your Ref: 1004/*L*

The Inside Address

This is the address of the person to whom the letter is directed, and it is typed from the left-hand margin, two or three spaces below the date and reference line. It may be in *block form*:

> The Personnel Manager,
> Wright Engineering Company,
> 53 Macclesfield Street,
> Steepley, Yorks.

or *indented form*:

> The Personnel Manager,
> Wright Engineering Company,
>   53 Macclesfield Street,
>   Steepley, Yorks.

Where possible the address should be confined to three or four lines.

There should be consistency in the use of one particular form. Use the same form on the envelope as you have used in the letter.

The address should be correctly punctuated—full stops after abbreviations where necessary, and commas separating the various parts of the address. A comma is not essential after the street number.

Use *Mr.* or *Esq.* for a single person—*e.g.*,

Mr. R. A. Jones or *R. A. Jones Esq.*

Use *Esq.* if there are letters to follow the man's name, and always make sure that the initials are given.

Messrs is seldom used nowadays, except for addressing two or more people—*e.g.*, Messrs Smith and Brown. Limited companies, being impersonal, are *not* so addressed, and if the letter is not directed to a specific person such as the Sales Manager, Works Manager, or Managing Director, it should be addressed to the Secretary—*e.g.*,

The Secretary,
Smith and Brown Ltd.

N.B. In personal letters, and in such formal letters as those applying for posts, the inside address is usually at the bottom left of the letter.

Salutation and Complimentary Close

SALUTATION	COMPLIMENTARY CLOSE
1. Dear Sir, Dear Sirs, (Dear) Madam, Mesdames,	Yours faithfully, Yours truly,
2. Sir, Gentlemen, Madam, Mesdames,	Your obedient servant, Yours respectfully,
3. Dear Mr . . . . ., Dear Mrs . . . . ., Dear Miss . . . . ., Dear . . . . .,	Yours sincerely, Yours truly,

The first form is the one usually employed in business letters. The second form is that used in more formal correspondence—official reports and memos, government correspondence, etc. The third form involves the only use of *Yours sincerely* in business letters and is used when the writer is acquainted with the person addressed. You will, however, find several slight variations in practice.

N.B. *I remain* and other linking phrases are used only after a participle construction at the end of the letter—*e.g.*,

Hoping you will deal with this immediately,

I remain,
Yours faithfully,

It is then essential to the correct grammatical construction. Such a form is, however, clumsy, and *you should try to avoid it*. It is better to write:

> *I hope you will deal with this immediately.*
>
> *Yours faithfully,*

You should be familiar with the reference book which contains the special forms of address (see section on reference work)—*i.e.*, letters addressed to Dukes, Bishops, etc.

The Body of the Letter

This should be written in clear and concise English with correct paragraphing and punctuation. Full-stops, commas, and question marks are the important marks in letter-writing and should be used sparingly to convey exactness of meaning and to avoid ambiguity.

Each paragraph should express a separate item in the letter, and may consist merely of a sentence; but too many short paragraphs can spoil the appearance of the letter. There are conventional ways of paragraphing, examples of which will be given in the next section.

The use of *inst.*, *ult.*, and *prox.* is still common, but is not good practice—better to put the date in full and avoid any possible misunderstanding.

inst.	this month
ult.	last month
prox.	next month

In letters of reply the opening paragraph is a conventional one and the following opening phrases are suggested as positive means of avoiding jargon:

> In reply to your letter of . . .
> With reference to your letter of . . .
> In answer to your letter of . . .
> Thank you for your letter of . . .
> With reference to your advertisement in . . . of . . .
> Confirming our conversation of . . .
> Confirming our telephone conversation of . . .
> Thank you for your order of . . .
> We have received your order of . . .
> With reference to your enquiry of . . .

The following are examples of errors which are frequently made by commercial students in their exercises. They can be avoided with care and concentration:

AVOID:

the phrase *Believe me to be*
the phrase *Thanking you in anticipation*
careless composition (this shows disrespect)
mis-spelling (use a reference book)
mixing the pronouns *I* and *we*
misplaced phrases and unrelated participles
interlining for material omitted
repetition of *I* or *We* at the beginning of paragraphs
the use of the imperative (this creates a bad tone)
an incomplete opening paragraph—*e.g.*, *With reference to your letter of the 15th April.* (no main verb)
the abbreviation *advert.* (Write it in full.)

REMEMBER:

to refer to previous correspondence where necessary
the rules for word-division
indention for paragraphs
to use a subject-heading where helpful

B. Types of Business Letter

The following notes and examples cover only a small part of the subject and are intended merely as a guide in these preliminary stages. The suggestions for paragraphing are not rules but aids to letter-writing.

1. *Ordering Goods*

All the relevant information should be given and shown clearly. Tabulate the items if necessary.

PARAGRAPHING

(*a*) Reference to source of information.
(*b*) List of goods required. Include quantity, quality, price, catalogue references, etc.
(*c*) Details of delivery and payment.

PRICE ELECTRICS

14 HIGH STREET
BARCHESTER

12th May, 19..

The Sales Manager,
Lumex Ltd.,
Grays Street,
London, E.C.4.

Dear Sir,

Fluorescent light fittings

    Thank you for your letter of the 9th May, and for the enclosed catalogue. Will you please supply the following light fittings:

	£	s.	d.
One 5ft twin louvred fitting No. 349	10	7	—
Two 4ft louvred fittings with tapped control gear No. 261	15	9	—
Three twin 5ft mesh-sided fittings No. 57	58	7	—
	£84	3	—
Less 5% Discount	4	4	—
	£79	19	—

    I shall be glad if these items can be delivered as soon as possible.

Yours faithfully,

Manager

2. *Acknowledgements*

An indication of business courtesy. An acknowledgement may be made by letter or by printed card. When payment is involved, an official receipt should be sent promptly with the acknowledgement.

EXAMPLE

(*a*)

```
              SMITH & JONES LTD

                              Coombe Way,
                              Hertford.
                              . . . . . . . . . .

Dear.....
     Thank you for your..........of...
....... which is receiving our careful
attention.

                    Yours  truly,
```

(*b*)

```
              Stantforth College

                              Bocking,
                              Essex.
                              . . . . . . .

    The Principal thanks you for your
application which will receive early
consideration.

    You will be given further informa-
tion as soon as possible.
```

3. *Covering Letter*

A short letter enclosing a form, typescript, or publication which is virtually self-explanatory. Sometimes a compliment slip is used for this purpose.

EXAMPLE

(a)

TRISTEEL BOILER CO.

LODGE STREET
LONDON, E.C.1

14th September, 19..

E. B. James Esq.,
Steye Walk,
Chelmsford, Essex.

Dear Sir,

With reference to your letter of
the 12th September, I enclose a
catalogue of our domestic boilers.
Further information and advice are
available at any time through our
Personal Advisory Service.

Yours faithfully,

Enc.   Sales Manager

(b)

TRISTEEL BOILER CO.

Lodge Street,
London, E.C.1.

With the compliments

of the

Sales Manager

4. *Letter of Enquiry*

Such letters vary from a request for a catalogue to a confidential letter asking for information about an employee. They are usually short and to the point, stating what is required in clear and unambiguous terms.

EXAMPLE

(a)

13 Grove Road,
London, S.E.19.

12th May, 19..

The Manager,
Forsythe Nurseries,
Salisbury, Wilts.

Dear Sir,

Several years ago I bought from you a selection of rockery plants. They have proved very successful, and I now wish to add to my collection. Please let me know whether you are able to supply new varieties.

Yours faithfully,

C

(b)

HEBDON & SMITH LTD

STATION ROAD,
LONDON, S.W.14

Ref: LAK/TM   11th November, 19..

Personal & Confidential

The Personnel Manager,
Platt Engineering Co.,
Fordham, Bucks.

Dear Sir,

John Henry Wright

The above-named has applied to us for the job of foreman in our processing department.

He tells us that, for the period January 19.. to March 19.., he worked as a chargehand in a similar department of your engineering company, before he moved to his present employment.

We should appreciate confirmation of this fact and your comments upon his suitability for a responsible post. Any such information will, of course, be treated in strict confidence.

Yours faithfully,

Works Manager

5. *Complaints*

An initial letter of complaint should be a tactful, carefully-worded statement. There may be a perfectly good reason for the mistake, or the person offending may be unaware of the effects of his action and be quite willing to do something about it. The tone of the letter should be calm and dignified, with no tempers lost or use of dire threats.

PARAGRAPHING

 (*a*) reference to source of complaint
 (*b*) its origin and effects
 (*c*) request for action

EXAMPLE

14th May, 19..

The Secretary,
Selwood Shoe Co. Ltd.,
Norwich.

Dear Sir,

Order No. 778/9

 On the 19th March you sent me a consignment of men's shoes, invoiced at 87/6d a pair, which were advertised in your catalogue as first-quality foot-wear made from the best leather.

 The shoes that were delivered did not come up to the standard claimed for them, but followed closely the specification in your catalogue for cheaper-quality shoes at 47/6d a pair.

 As my business is concerned with expensive footwear of good quality, I am returning the consignment and ask that you replace it with the correct quality.

Yours faithfully,

If no satisfaction is obtained from the first letter, a second complaint will be necessary, stronger in tone but maintaining tact and dignity.

PARAGRAPHING

    (*a*) reference to other firm's letter (or to your previous letter if it has evoked no reply)
    (*b*) explanation of lack of satisfaction
    (*c*) warning of steps that may have to be taken. (This does not involve threats.)

N.B. (*a*) In certain circumstances you should enclose a copy of your previous letter. (*b*) Remember that legal action is the last step and should not be taken until all alternative actions have been tried.

EXAMPLE

1st June, 19..

```
The Secretary,
Selwood Shoe Co. Ltd.,
Norwich.

Dear Sir,

            Order No. 778/9

     With reference to my letter of the
14th May, in which I notified you of
the return of a consignment of shoes,
I must inform you that I have so far
received no reply to that letter, nor
have I received a credit note for the
goods returned.

     I would remind you that the order
was placed in good faith, but that the
goods supplied were well below specifi-
cation.  It was, therefore, only
reasonable that I should return them
```

with a request for replacement. Should
you be unable to replace, I must ask
you to cancel the order.

Yours faithfully,

If money were involved in this transaction, a further paragraph would be needed to warn the shoe company of the
possibility of legal action to recover the sum.

6. *Introductions*

The representative of a firm may need a letter of introduction
when visiting another organization, or he may be given a
general letter of introduction which will explain his duties to
any person whom he meets in the course of business.

PARAGRAPHING

    (*a*) formal introduction of person bearing the letter
    (*b*) details of that person—qualifications, etc.
    (*c*) any facilities requested

EXAMPLE

    (*a*)

12th April, 19..
The Managing Director,
Burg & Bowen Ltd.,
Manchester.

Dear Sir,

The bearer of this letter, Mr
William E. Jones, is one of our sales
representatives.

He has recently been concerned
with opening markets for our goods on
the Continent, and with the establishing of agencies at Channel ports. He

is now negotiating, on our behalf, the purchase of lightweight packing materials for cross-Channel shipments.

We shall be grateful if you will give him all the help and advice you can.

Yours faithfully,

(*b*)

11th October, 19..

To whom it may concern:

James Richards is acting as a representative of the "Thornton News."

I should appreciate any help you could give him in the carrying out of his duties.

Editor

7. *Apology*

This should not be so overwritten as to become servile in tone. Apologize once, that is sufficient—the intention to make amends is more important.

PARAGRAPHING

(*a*) reference to source (*e.g.*, letter of complaint)
(*b*) explanation of cause (but do not pass the blame on to a subordinate)
(*c*) intended action
(*d*) apology

N.B. Instead of being in the last paragraph, the apology may introduce the letter.

EXAMPLE

3rd June, 19..

The Sales Manager,
G. Smith & Co. Ltd.,
High Street,
Fordham.

Dear Sir,

Order No. 778/9

We have received your letter of
the 1st June, stating that we had not
acknowledged your previous letter and
the return of a consignment of shoes.

Your original letter was received,
and we discovered that the consignment
sent to you had been wrongly labelled.
The high-quality shoes you required
were not available, and we wrote on the
16th May explaining that replacement
was impossible for at least eight
weeks. A copy of that letter is enclosed. Since that time we have been
waiting for your instructions, unaware
that our letter had not been received.

Replacement should be possible
within the next fortnight, but we will
cancel the order if you consider the
delay too long.

We thank you for the return of the
consignment, and regret the inconvenience caused by the mistake.

Yours faithfully,

Enc.   Manager

8. *Invitations and Replies*

Formal invitations are usually phrased in the third person. When required in quantity they are usually printed, but for small official functions typed invitations are more economical. Inside address, salutation, and complimentary close are omitted.

EXAMPLES

(*a*) Invitation:

15 Styles Walk,
London, S.W.3

Mr. & Mrs. J. Jones request the pleasure of

. . . . *company at an exhibition of water-colour*

painting to be held at . . . . *on Saturday,*

12th May, 19.. at 2.30 p.m.

R.S.V.P.

(*b*) Reply:

13 Grand Drive,
London, S.E.4.

Mr. R. Robinson thanks Mr. and Mrs. Jones for their kind invitation to ....at........on.......but regrets that he cannot be present because of a previous engagement.

9. *Applications*

In the early stages of one's career, the relevant information can be given in the body of the letter.

PARAGRAPHING

(*a*) reference to source and formal application
(*b*) age and education (to school-leaving age)

(c) further education and appropriate subjects

(d) previous employment

(e) any other experience or qualification useful for the post

(f) enclosure of testimonials and details of referees

(g) concluding sentence

N.B. This letter will, of course, be *handwritten*.

EXAMPLE

16th March, 19..

Dear Sir,

I wish to apply for the post of Secretary which you advertised in the "Daily News" of the 14th March.

I am 19 years of age and was educated at the Stapleigh Girls' Grammar School, where I obtained six passes in the General Certificate of Education.

After leaving school I took a two-year course at Stapleigh College of Commerce, where I studied Commercial subjects and passed Royal Society of Arts examinations in shorthand and typewriting at speeds of, respectively, 80 and 35 words per minute. I also passed the Intermediate examination of the Chartered Institute of Secretaries, in English, Secretarial Practice, and Economics.

My present duties are as Private Secretary to the Managing Director of an engineering firm, and my work has involved not only the normal secretarial responsibilities, but also the preparation of technical material for publication.

The following persons have agreed
to give references on my behalf:

R. Boulton Esq., Rook Engineering,
    Tolworth, Surrey.
Rev. J. Galt, Brookside, Ashtead,
    Surrey.

If my application is considered I
shall be available for interview at any
time.

Yours faithfully,

The Advertiser,
Box 763,
"The Daily News,"
London, E.C.1.

As you progress in your career, and possibly gain further
qualifications as well as increased experience, you may have to
give these details in an enclosure and not in the body of the
letter. Such information may be typed and sent with a
handwritten covering letter.

EXAMPLE

Dear Sir,

In applying for the post of
Personal Secretary to the Manager, I
enclose a typescript giving details of
my qualifications and experience. From
this you will see that most of my
experience as a personal secretary has
been with engineering firms, involving
the preparation of technical reports
and publications.

If you consider that my qualifications are suitable, I shall be available for interview at any time.

Yours faithfully,

<u>Details of Qualifications and</u>

<u>Experience of Miss Rachel Smith</u>

Age: 30 years.

Education:
    Stapleigh Girls' Grammar School
      19.. to 19..
      (G.C.E. in 7 subjects, incl.
    French, General Science, and
    Applied Maths.)
    Stapleigh College of Commerce,
      19.. to 19..
      (R.S.A. Shorthand/Typing Stage
    III.)
      (C.I.S. Inter, English, Secre-
    tarial Practice, Economics,
    Company Law, Accountancy,
    Principles of Law.)

Experience:
    19.. to 19..   Rook Engineering,
                    Tolworth, Surrey.
                    Private Secretary.
    19.. to 19..   Palmer & Jones,
                    14 Smith Street,
                    London, E.C.4.
                    Secretary to Chief
                    Consultant.

Present Employment:

from 19..   Gower Engineering
Ltd., Chesham,
Bucks. Private
Secretary to the
Manager.

Duties:

Normal secretarial duties, plus
summarizing of technical reports
and preparation of material for
the printers. Presentation of
statistical material.

References:

Rev. J. Galt, Brookside, Ashtead,
Surrey.

A. J. Jones, Palmer & Jones, 14
Smith Street, E.C.4.

P. R. Hewitt, Gower Engineering
Ltd., Chesham, Bucks.

10. *Circular Letters*

These are usually cyclostyled or printed and are intended for more than one addressee. Their purpose is to give information or to gain custom.

(*a*) GIVING INFORMATION

Routine letters such as notification of temporary breaks in public services, alterations in rates or prices, dates and particulars of meetings, etc. This type of circular letter also includes the stock printed replies to enquiries. The essential qualities are clarity and complete lack of ambiguity.

EXAMPLE

Dear Sir or Madam,

Increase in Rates of Interest

    At a recent meeting of the Board it was decided that the following increased interest rates should come into effect from 1st September, 19..:

Deposit Accounts	$4\frac{1}{2}$% per annum
Other Accounts	5% per annum

The Society will arrange to pay the Income Tax in all instances.

    In view of the continuing need for personal saving, and the urgent appeal made recently by the Government, we hope that the new rates of interest will stimulate investment. Our report for the last financial year showed a steady increase in deposits, a healthy sign which encouraged the Society to announce the improved rates.

    Despite this decision to raise the interest rates, the Board has been able to avoid a corresponding increase in the rates charged to borrowers. This has only been possible because of the careful action taken in the past and through the support given by our investors. We are confident that such support will be maintained.

            Yours faithfully,

A circular letter giving information about a forthcoming meeting may dispense with the salutation. It usually includes the Agenda of the Meeting.

BATTERBY BOWLING CLUB

Hon. Sec. P. B. May,
    14 Stein Road,
    Batterby.
Tel. Batterby 43.

FORTH ROAD,
BATTERBY.

14th April, 19..

NOTICE OF MEETING

The Annual General Meeting of the Club will be held at the Batterby Church Hall on Friday 25th April, at 7.30 p.m. The President, Mr F. H. Smith, will be in the chair.

AGENDA

1. Minutes of previous A.G.M.
2. Matters arising from the minutes
3. Chairman's report
4. Treasurer's report
5. Election of officers
6. Repairs to pavilion
7. Any other business

P. B. May

Hon. Secretary

(*b*) SEEKING CUSTOM

In recent years this has developed into a special technique and has become increasingly the task of professional advertisers. But, in spite of the special printing devices, the vouchers and

the tricks of psychology, there are a few simple rules that
govern any circular letter.

1. It should be well written.
2. It must show good reasons for being sent.
3. The reader's attention must be caught in the first sentence.
4. It must come to the point quickly.

As with any other letter the reader should be the prime
consideration.

EXAMPLE

Dear Madam,

    Have you noticed how small your
kitchen seems?

    Even if you are lucky enough to
work in a reasonable kitchen area, can
you really say that you have room to
move freely? There are those chairs
that get in your way, the sharp corners
that dig into your ribs as you pass,
the cupboard doors left dangerously
open. Minor irritants perhaps, but
sufficient to make you long for a
larger kitchen.

    Yet you have the answer without
moving. Even the tiniest kitchen can
be made tolerable by careful planning.
Stackway Kitchen Fittings give you
ample storage with the maximum freedom
of movement, simply by making full use
of the wall space and enabling you to
reach those high, normally inaccessible
cupboard areas. There are no ladders
necessary; instead, a system of self-
lowering shelves, quick and simple to
operate, takes the stretching out of
storing.

We do not pretend that our kitchen
units are cheap, but the ingenious
metal framework used in their construction enables a kitchen to be equipped
in several stages, and according to the
family budget. We plan your kitchen
for you, without charge, and you order
the units when you require them.

The enclosed catalogue will give
you a general idea of the design of our
fittings; the planning is an individual service in which we treat each
kitchen according to its size and
shape. We welcome any enquiries. Just
detach the reply card from the catalogue and post it to us so that we may
have the pleasure of helping you.

Yours truly,

N.B. The above notes and examples are only a *guide* to
letter-writing. You will find in practice that some letters will
not fit those patterns, and must be composed according to the
particular circumstances. The basic principle of simple,
straightforward English remains the same, and your success
will still depend upon consideration of that important person
—the ultimate reader of your letter. What does he want to
know, and how can you explain it to him clearly and concisely?

STANDARD FORM

Many firms have introduced methods of dealing promptly
with routine correspondence. Printed acknowledgement post-
cards and compliment slips save the time of both employer and
secretary; but the method is limited. Printed letters answering
enquiries can be too impersonal, at a stage of the business when
a sense of personal attention is needed.

The correspondence of a firm dealing in a particular section
of trade tends to become repetitive. Orders or enquiries from
customers require similar replies, and, as a means of saving

valuable time, such firms have developed *standard letter forms*. A suitably phrased letter is composed to meet certain requirements and is then filed with other standard letters under a specific reference number. The executive, instead of dictating a letter, can quote the reference and leave his secretary to type it from the file copy.

To avoid such letters becoming stereotyped in style and tone, standard form can be restricted to paragraphs similarly numbered and filed. The executive can then dictate part of the letter and give a reference for a particular paragraph to be added. In this way the personal tone of the letter is safeguarded.

C. **Tone**

You have been told that a letter should be concisely and clearly expressed, and this is not difficult to achieve in routine letters; but you will sometimes be faced with letters requiring more careful thought and consideration—letters demanding tact and a special approach to the persons who will read them. It is then that the *way* you write the letter becomes increasingly important, and the problem of *tone* is not an easy one.

In spoken English, tone (the modulation of the voice by inflexion and intonation) comes so naturally that we rarely stop to analyse it. We raise the voice in anger, or by rising inflexion ask a question; the voice quickens its rhythm in moments of impatience, or takes a bitter tone in an outburst of sarcasm. Try to convert this to the written word and the problem seems insuperable. In desperation, the writer resorts to exclamation marks or to underlining, but these are poor substitutes. Yet tone is important in letter-writing—even if there is no need for extremes of emotional expression—and there are several ways of conveying it to a reader.

Vocabulary

Words have not only meaning but connotation and atmosphere. Simple onomatopoeic words such as *murmur, hiss,* and *click* suggest sound as well as meaning; short words such as *pig, stupid,* and *crass* have an insulting tone; *shiver, horror,* and *smudge* suggest feeling in a more subtle way; *edifice, garb,* and *impecunious* have an air of false gentility; *cool, balm, smooth* are words that have a soothing quality; *quick, snatch, stop* suggest a peremptory tone. If words can have such an emotional quality, it is obviously important to make a correct choice, and to avoid creating a wrong impression.

Letter-writing requires a direct but polite tone. Words such as *please, grateful, thank you, personal, appreciate,* do much to create the right atmosphere; on the other hand, if they are carelessly used, *obvious, wrong, mistaken, simple* can contribute to a brusque and rude tone.

The wish to appear important often reveals itself in the use of pedestrian Latinisms and an overfondness for abstract nouns: a ceremony cannot be important unless it *commences,* rather than *begins;* instead of *receiving* a letter, the person addressed becomes *the recipient.* Such words as *commences* and *recipient* do indeed create a tone—one of pompousness—but the reader is seldom impressed. Use simple, straightforward words that express your meaning clearly and courteously, and that show you to be natural and sincere.

Sentences

The tone of a letter depends partly upon the length and structure of the sentences and paragraphs. In general, shortness gives a suggestion of briskness; lengthiness develops a more restful tone. But an extreme use of a particular type can be dangerous. A letter consisting chiefly of short sentences may give an air of rudeness rather than of brisk efficiency; a series of long sentences may make a letter turgid and pompous. The answer is, of course, variation of sentence length, with a preponderance of short sentences. There is seldom any need for complicated sentence building in letter writing.

Writing a letter is not a literary task, and you should avoid the literary style. Subtly contrived complex and compound sentences are rarely necessary—unless in letters requiring great tact—and you should prefer the *loose* to the *periodic* sentence. The section on Sentence Structure (p. 164) will give you further advice.

Letter paragraphs are usually short and to the point, but a succession of very short paragraphs can suggest curtness and even rudeness, as well as appearing ludicrous on the typed page. Lengthy paragraphs have a formidable appearance, and give an initial impression of dullness.

The Verb

The correct use of the verb has an important influence upon tone. A business letter should be direct, but will have little chance if most of its verbs are in the passive voice. The terms *active* and *passive* are well chosen, and the use of the active voice means an unequivocal statement with the verb linked clearly to the subject. Although the passive voice may, in some instances, suggest objectivity, more often than not it results in vagueness of expression.

"If we were to do this work," with its active verb, has a more direct and reasonable tone than "If this work were to be done by us," with its tortuous use of the passive.

The use of the imperative gives a definite tone to a letter, often when that tone is not intended: "If you wish to order any items from our catalogue, use the enclosed business reply card." The peremptory tone of the imperative "use" is unsuited to what is, after all, a request and not a demand. The simple courtesy of "please" before the imperative would soften the tone; the phrase "will you please use" would efface any suggestion of a demand.

Here is one last piece of advice about tone. Think less about how the letter appears and sounds to you, and more about how it will affect the reader.

D. Commercial Jargon

The use of the term 'Commercial English' in text-books and curricula has, unfortunately, perpetuated the idea that there is a special form of English for letter-writing. This exclusiveness has, even more unfortunately, been associated with Commercial Jargon—that ugly, conventional way of writing identified by such phraseology as:

> It is incumbent upon me to take the matter in hand.
> In re yours of the 5th inst.
> We are the recipients of your favour of yesterday's date.

These are extreme examples which have been ridiculed out of common use, but there are still many examples of circumlocution and turgidity in business correspondence to-day, and such is the power of these fossilized statements that it is not always easy for the student to avoid them. Look at the following list and the 'translations' given. Learn to recognize jargon and avoid it.

We are in receipt of your favour We are the recipients of your letter We beg to acknowledge receipt of your letter In re your letter Your favour to hand	With reference to your letter Thank you for your letter We have received your letter
It is incumbent upon us	We must
It is felt to be necessary	We think it necessary
It will be our earnest endeavour	We shall try
It has been brought to our notice	We have noticed
It is within my power	I can
It is our opinion	We think

(and similar constructions *ad nauseam*)

on the upgrade	increasing, improving
wholly unfounded	untrue
communicate	write, send
in our possession	we have
on Tuesday next	next Tuesday
despatch	send
the same, same	it
furnish	give, provide
purchase	buy
your favour	your letter
at your convenience	when convenient
commence	begin
I have enclosed I enclose herewith Enclosed please find	I enclose
a percentage of a proportion of	some
We beg to assure you	We assure you
We are wholly at a loss to understand	We cannot understand
We have instituted the necessary enquiries	We are enquiring
We shall take a very early opportunity of writing	We shall write soon

We are of the opinion that	We think that
We are desirous of	We wish
We are prepared to offer	We offer (or, will offer)
We are obliged to	We must, we have to
upward movement in prices	rise in prices
consequent upon	because of, as a result of
your good selves	you
in view of the fact that	since

Compare this letter:

Dear Sir,

We beg to acknowledge the receipt of your letter of the 15th inst., in which you brought to our notice a decrease in sales consequent upon the recent upward movement in prices.

It is felt that your expression of concern at this untoward situation is unwarranted as the decrease is, in our opinion, merely of a temporary nature. Should, however, the situation become worse we shall do everything in our power to effect a reduction in certain prices where possible.

Yours faithfully,

with the following version:

Dear Sir,

Thank you for your letter of the 15th of this month, informing us of the drop in sales following recent price increases.

We think you are worrying needlessly over a temporary setback, but should it continue we shall seriously consider reducing certain prices.

Yours faithfully,

Which is the more direct? Which is the easier to read and understand? Notice how the abstract nouns and passive constructions have been altered, and the circumlocutions avoided.

E. Converting Commercial Jargon

Convert each of the following phrases and sentences into clear and concise English:

1. in re yours of the 5th ult.
   the recent upward move in prices
   pending the finalizing of arrangements
   to make an inspection

2. I beg to acknowledge the receipt of your favour in which was given the date of commencement of the plan.

3. We are the recipients of your favour of the 15th ult., and wish to inform you that the same will receive our best attention.

4. It has been brought to our notice that the representative sent to your residence was not accorded the hospitality he expected.

5. It will be our earnest endeavour to carry out the requests stated in your order, and we shall immediately despatch such goods as are in our possession.

6. If you will communicate to us the results of those enquiries instituted by you, we shall be only too pleased to furnish all particulars.

7. It is not without some temerity that I venture to submit a criticism of the report, but I feel that it is incumbent upon me to do so.

8. If it is within my power to put forward recommendations for instituting severe disciplinary action against recalcitrant employees, I shall make every effort to do so.

9. I feel bound to point out that the duty of inspecting the machinery for the exchange of personnel is within your purview and is, therefore, your responsibility.

10. It is felt that your remarks are not without some foundation, but pending the finalization of the arrangements we are still desirous of pursuing some temporary course of action.

11. We beg to advise you that, contrary to all expectations, there has occurred a severe depreciation in the value of your stock, and it will be to your advantage to rid yourself of what is virtually a liability by a sale of that stock.

12. In the light of experience which extends over a good many years, it is our opinion that the upward trend in prices will not continue for any length of time.

13. As the result of a sequence of abstruse calculations, it has been computed mathematically that personnel fatigue varies according to stages in the daily schedule.

14. In consequence of your precipitate action, it is felt to be necessary that a safeguard be put upon the carrying-out of decisions by members of the Board of Directors without prior consultation with other members, thus ensuring that there is unanimous responsibility.

15. In re your enquiry of recent date we have instituted the necessary investigation and shall take an early opportunity of informing you of the result. In consequence of the error in despatch of your goods we shall expedite the replacement with goods of a more suitable quality.

F. Exercises in the Arrangement and Punctuation of Letters

1. 13 farmhouse lane digby notts 13th september 19.. foster nurseries plimpton lincs dear sirs with reference to your advertisement in the daily news of 10th september i wish to place the following order for spring bulbs 3 doz pinchams purple glory @ 5/- per doz 15s 2 doz dightons parrot tulips red and white @ 4/6 per doz 9s 4 doz blue riband hyacinths @ 5/- per doz £1 total £2 4s i enclose cheque for £2 7 which includes 3/- carriage yours faithfully a pitt

2. briggs publications ltd portway house e c 4 15th april 19.. b dingleby esq torway wincing lane rigby hants dear mr dingleby artifacts of the south downs thank you for your ms on the above subject it has received careful attention from our reader who was impressed by the scholarship shown we must however point out that the books we publish are for the general market and such a work would not be suitable for our catalogue there are however specialist publishers who would be more likely to accept the ms for publication and we recommend that you submit it to breen and co of purchase street s w 9 your ms is being returned under separate cover yours sincerely roger dunne managing editor

3. woodsmith garage high street marston march 19.. the occupier dear sir now that spring is approaching have you considered the state of your car especially in view of the extra work it will do when the brighter weather comes cars often need as careful attention as human beings after a hard winter and you cannot do better than bring your car to our garage for servicing perhaps as a result of your visit to the motor show you are thinking of buying a new model here we can also be of great help for we are agents for a number of the prominent companies several of the latest models can be seen in our show

rooms and a demonstration car is always available take a trip in the car you fancy why not come along and discuss with our manager the part-exchange of your older model whatever your motoring needs the woodsmith garage is always at your service sincerely yours j brown director

4. mr and mrs edward byng request the pleasure of mr james fortunes company at a dinner party to be given on the occasion of their sons coming of age on 13th june 19.. at the melbourne hotel porchester 7 for 7 30 p m r s v p

5. 13 sharpes avenue cardiff 15th april 19.. e p wilkes f a l p a charter house phipps street cardiff dear sir plot 9 hill garden estate with reference to your letter of the 12th may in which you informed me that development charges would be payable on the above site i should like further information about any other charges anticipated in connexion with the construction of the house i have given instructions for the builders to begin the first stage but will not cancel this unless i receive your advice to do so with many thanks for your assistance i remain yours truly j smith

6. 15 high street bingham 1st november 19.. dear sirs with reference to your advertisement in the bingham news i wish to apply for the post of warehouseman i am 30 years of age and was educated at bingham central school where i gained school leaving certificate and followed my normal education with part time classes in bookkeeping at bingham technical college for the past 10 years i have been employed as a ledger clerk with messrs boot and sons of bingham the following people have agreed to give references on my behalf the rev j smithers the vicarage bingham t a boot esq manager messrs boot and sons bingham should i be selected i shall do my best to justify your choice yours faithfully a j swain wootten engineering co ltd 15 frith street bingham

7. smiths mills bradford yorks 18th april 19.. haj 235 farnsworth and co ltd wholesale clothiers 15 west street london e c 4 dear sirs consignments of wool cloth thank you for your letter of the 15th april enquiring about types of woollen cloth available for suit manufacture we have pleasure in forwarding patterns of the latest materials as follows serge unshrinkable and fast dye 54 in in 20 yd pieces @ 12/- a yard ordinary woollen serge slightly lower grade 54 in pieces @ 9/- a yard

stocks of these materials are reasonable and we are able to offer 5% discount on more than 10 pieces yours faithfully j b smith for smiths mills

8. council offices bradbury 15th july 19.. t brown esq orchard lane bradbury dear sir i have received your letter of the 12th july referring to the compulsory purchase order applied to your property and have discussed the matter with the town planning officer unfortunately there is no way of replanning the main road to avoid your property but the following suggestions were made a that the road be curved to cross three acre field this would involve expensive banking b that part of the council owned land on the other side of your farm be conveyed to you in the purchase to compensate for loss of arable land either scheme would avoid hardship but this is the only compromise that seems possible i regret that we are unable to do anything more but i know that the town planning officer will be pleased to discuss with you any plans for reducing interference with your work yours faithfully w greene town clerk

9. walter grellan & co solicitors 15 place street e c 4 ref sdb/54 13th may 19.. d barnby esq portia lodge crickleham wilts dear sir 12 church lane medham with reference to the recent agreement signed by you in respect of the above property i suggest that a further clause be added to cover sub tenancy mr wilbur the vendor is agreeable and has seen the entry which is enclosed for your approval and signature the addition of the new clause automatically requires deletion of the entry on page 3 of the agreement beginning letting of the aforesaid property and ending without the owners consent the early return of the form would be appreciated yours faithfully t f mackeson for walter grellan & co

10. the cressing sports club dover road cressing kent 15th october 19.. r jones the drive cressing kent dear mr jones the annual general meeting of this club will be held in the club house on friday 28th october at 7 30 p m the vice president mr j watts smith will be in the chair and the agenda for the meeting will be as follows 1 minutes of previous a g m 2 matters arising 3 chairmans report 4 treasurers report 5 election of officers 6 resolution that the constitution be amended to permit the admission of part time members on payment of a special

fee such fee to be decided at a special meeting of the membership sub committee proposed by mr k wright seconded by mr
o rigby 7 a o b the committee asks members to show their
support by making this year's meeting a record one yours
sincerely a booth secretary

G. Rephrasing and Re-casting Letters

The following letters are poorly composed and contain
examples of verbosity, jargon, poor sentence structure, and
clumsy paragraphing. Rewrite each letter in a clear and
concise manner, retaining the letter form. In some instances
you may have to rearrange the order of items in the letter, but
be careful not to alter the basic meaning.

I.

THE MEDFORD LITERARY SOCIETY

> HON. SEC. P. N. GRANT,
> FOURWAYS,
> MEDFORD, SUSSEX.

14th August, 19..

R. B. Petworth Esq., Ph.D., F.S.A.,
Bramble Cottage,
Belford, Sussex.

Dear Sir,

      The Society, who are now in the
process of considering the programme
for their winter session, have
requested me on their behalf, to ask
whether you will be prepared to deliver
a lecture some time during January or
February of next year. Medford is not

too inconvenient for you, being on the
main line from London and providing an
easy connexion at Garston Junction.
The journey should not take more than
an hour.

The members of the Society have
frequently expressed a desire to invite
a visiting speaker who is an expert in
Anglo Saxon studies. As you will no
doubt know, there have been a number of
interesting archaeological discoveries
in the vicinity and local interest is
of a strong nature.

Our Society has been in existence
for over fifty years and its membership
is still on the increase. We are of
the opinion that you will have a
stimulating audience.

It had come to our notice that you
were interested in delivering lectures
to societies such as ours, and we
should appreciate the opportunity of
listening to an expert dissertation on
the ways of our "rude forefathers."
You can rest assured that all your
expenses will be paid.

The Society is accustomed to meet
every Saturday evening at 7.30 p.m. in
the Town Hall. Let us know if you will
be able to manage a Saturday evening in
January or February. We leave the
choice of subject to you, but send the
title when you can so that it can be
announced in our winter prospectus.
You will be expected to speak for about
ninety minutes, after which there will

be an opportunity for questions and
discussion by the audience.

We hope you will be able to come.

Yours faithfully,

Hon. Sec.

2.

SYKES & STONEHAM
Solicitors

15 THEOBALDS ROAD,
TADDENHAM,
SURREY.

12th April, 19..

A. F. French Esq.,
45 Duke Street,
Taddenham, Surrey.

Dear Sir,

In re 32 Manor Way, Taddenham

We beg to acknowledge receipt of
your letter of the 10th instant, concerning the purchase of the above
property, and note the remarks made by
you in regard to the decorative condition of the said property. While we
are in agreement regarding to comparative dilapidation of the roof, we are
wholly at a loss to understand your
comments upon the state of the interior
of the house which we consider to be in
a reasonable state of repair.

Consequent upon your letter it was considered desirable to communicate with the vendor's solicitors. This was effected immediately and we shall get in touch with you as soon as we have been furnished with all the necessary particulars.

We have already instituted the necessary enquiries with regard to the unmade road situate at the rear of the property, but it should be pointed out that any information supplied by the local authority will be of an indeterminate nature.

The fact that the roof requires re-tiling should have some influence upon the purchase price, and we are of the opinion that the vendor will agree to an adjustment. We do not consider, however, that he is likely to move in the matter of interior decoration, but we have, in our letter to the solicitors, raised the question on your behalf.

We would remind you that the vendor is pressing for signature of the contract and that it would be inadvisable to prolong the delay if you are really desirous of purchasing the house.

Yours faithfully,

for SYKES & STONEHAM

3.

BILBY'S

Tel. Melford 354, Ext. 6.
Carpet Dept.

HIGH STREET,
MELFORD,
KENT.

Your Ref: CY/34/D   15th June, 19..

The Sales Manager,
Newool Carpet Co.,
Kidderminster.

Dear Sir,

Referring to your letter of the 13th June and the consignment of goods despatched to us and arriving on 14th.

It is with regret that we have to report that certain of the items were damaged, namely three rugs, in transit by rail. The other rugs and rolls of carpeting had experienced a certain amount of ill treatment and were in varying degrees of dirtiness.

In view of the state in which the goods were received we felt it necessary to sign the appropriate documents only with a written and agreed statement as to their condition on arrival. Acceptance of the consignment was, therefore, acceptance of it in that condition.

The three rugs in question are damaged to such an extent as to be unsaleable.

The other items are less seriously affected and we are of the opinion that they can be cleaned without seriously affecting their value. We hope, however, that you realize such expenditure to be your responsibility.

It should be pointed out that the goods will be kept in our warehouse until such time as you may inform us of the action you intend to take.

The three extensively damaged rugs were part of an order for which we had been waiting some time, and it is considered desirable that any further lengthy waiting period should be avoided. We await the favour of your early reply, trusting that you will deal promptly with this matter.

Please find enclosed a report of the damage which we hope will be of help to you. We are prepared to return the consignment to you on receipt of your instructions.

Yours faithfully,

Carpet Dept.

4.

66 Theobalds Avenue,
Siddington,
Midshire.

25th November, 19..

The Clerk to the Council,
Town Hall,
Siddington.

Dear Sir,

A situation has arisen in this
district of Siddington to which I feel
your attention ought to be called. I
have complained of the nuisance to the
police but they seem powerless to deal
with it. I am therefore applying to
you as the police say it is a District
Council affair.

It concerns the piece of vacant
ground in Fellows Road where the land-
mine fell in 1942 and demolished so
many houses. For months the debris of
the houses remained in situ, though it
ought to have been cleared. But I
suppose labour was difficult to obtain
during the war. However the site of
the incident has now been levelled,
which is something done in the right
direction.

I should like to know whether
anything further is to be done with the
site. At present it is a totally
derelict piece of ground and is being

used as a dump for all sorts of rubbish
which brings me to the subject of my
complaint. During the summer children
play around this rubbish and their
screams and shouts are most disturbing
to those of us who are residents in
what used to be considered a select and
quiet area of the town.

The point is this - does the
Council intend to allow the site to be
built up again? If so, when? Meanwhile can some fencing be put up with a
notice to prohibit trespassers and
dumping? If the idea is to lay out a
playground, we should like to have the
fact made public so that we know where
we stand. There seems to be plenty of
money from the rates to spend on some
things which are called "increased
amenities" which are not so clearly
essential as maintaining the pleasant
character of what has always been known
as a good residential quarter, mainly
for retired people. A playground, if a
new one is needed, ought to be put
where there are more children in the
near-by houses.

I should be glad to know as soon
as possible what it is proposed to do.

Yours very truly,

[R.S.A. S.T.C. Stage II]

D

5.

> 22 Accrington Terrace,
> Dalesby,
> Yorks.
>
> 29th April, 1952.

Capel and Bolton Ltd.,
The Bargain Mart,
York.

Dear Sirs,

About a fortnight ago I saw in the
"Dalesby Advertiser" your advertisement
of women's dresses in large sizes. You
described them as made of print, but I
find the material is nothing like what
I always understood as print. It is
very thin and all the stiffness I am
sure would wash out at once so that it
would be as limp as a rag. As well as
that the pattern is only printed on one
side. What I mean is that hardly
anything shows on the wrong side and I
think that such poor printing would
fade very quickly. Such material is
hardly worth making up and even at your
low price it is a poor buy.

But the advertisement sounded so
good that I sent for one of these
dresses to see if they would be worth
having. To begin with I have had to
wait nearly a fortnight before it came
which seems absurd as I live only a
very little way from York. Then when

it did come it was very badly packed.
I do think you might have put something
stiff in the parcel instead of sending
it just pushed into an ordinary big
envelope.

The worst of it is that the dress
is not my size at all. I know I put
the right size on my order but you have
sent one much too large. It must have
the wrong figures printed on the tab in
the neck. 26 is my usual size but this
26 is much too large. The dress is no
use to me at all.

I sent the cut-out coupon with my
order in the first place but I am
enclosing another coupon with this
letter, from this week's "Advertiser,"
so that you can see how I filled in the
first one.

I am keeping this dress, as I have
paid for it, but will you please tell
me if one of your other sizes is the
right 26 according to other makes of
dresses. If it is, I should be obliged
if you will send me one in the same
pattern as the one I have which I will
then return.

I must say that I do not think
this is a very good advertisement to
send out dresses that do not fit.

Yours faithfully,

[R.S.A. S.T.C. Stage II]

H. **Composing Letters of Reply from Notes**

In each of the following exercises you are given a letter of enquiry that has been received by a certain person or organization. The brief notes given after each letter are intended as a framework for the reply. Using the information in the notes, make a rough draft of the letter, then type a fair copy on quarto paper with correct addresses, and neat display, leaving a space for signature. Your reply should contain between 100 and 150 words, but do not strain to achieve this maximum and sacrifice clarity for 'padding.'

Most of the notes either directly state or imply that additional information must be given, and this may involve a test of general knowledge. It is not sufficient to rephrase the notes to provide the content of your letters, neither should you make wild and ridiculous guesses at any reasons or prices that are to be stated. Apply your common sense to both the composition and content of your letter.

The notes for the reply can be used for shorthand dictation practice. The notes should be read to the class at the appropriate speed after the original letter has been studied carefully. The reply should then be drafted straight from the shorthand notes.

I.

18 Purbeck Drive,
Merriston,
Surrey.

15th May, 19..

The Wilson Motor Company,
Beach Street,
Merriston, Surrey.

Dear Sirs,

You recently repaired the clutch
of my Stanton car, DYX 373, for which
you have submitted a bill for twenty-
five pounds.

When I bought the car from you
last year, I understood that there was
a guarantee which covered such repairs
where they were the result of faulty
materials. The defect was not the
result of my negligence and occurred
during the guarantee period. I was,
unfortunately, unable to report this at
once as I was on vacation.

Will you please confirm that the
work was carried out under that
guarantee.

Yours faithfully,

P. T. Entworth

NOTES FOR THE REPLY:

The Manager asked his Secretary to inform Mr. Entworth
that the defect was reported to the garage after the date of

expiry of the guarantee and the repair should be paid for. However, as Mr. Entworth was a good customer, and in view of his inability to report the defect, the company would regard the repair as under the guarantee. The bill was to be returned.

2.

10 Riverside Way,
Chosby,
Herts.

15th May, 19..

The Borough Surveyor,
Chosby Borough Council,
Council Offices,
Cross Street, Chosby.

Dear Sir,

For the past week workmen have been taking up the road outside my house. The noise of pneumatic drills and other tools has been deafening and the situation is becoming unbearable.

The din continues beyond normal working hours, often well into the night, causing my two children great distress and loss of sleep.

I should like to know when the work is likely to finish and if it is necessary for the noise to continue to such a late hour.

Yours faithfully,

P. B. Smith

Notes for the Reply:

The Borough Surveyor told his typist to inform Mr. Smith that the Council regretted the inconvenience, but large-scale operations were being carried out to improve the sewage disposal system. He gave reasons for the long hours of work and said that little could be done in view of the urgency of the work. Riverside Way should be clear within about two weeks.

3.

> 14 Staines Crescent,
> Marlton,
> Marlshire.
>
> 20th April, 19..

Park Nurseries,
Storton, Lincs.

Dear Sirs,

On the 19th February, I ordered from your nurseries an assortment of rose bushes for which I paid £7. 10. 0. The order - No. P.N.33762 - was acknowledged on the 24th February, and some of the bushes were delivered a week later.

Since then I have received no other part of my order and would remind you that 4 bushes of the Christopher Stone variety are still to come. In view of the lateness of the season I should like prompt delivery of these roses while there is still time to plant them.

Yours faithfully,

R. A. Jones

Notes for the Reply:

The Manager, Mr. Swanson, sent a letter of apology to Mr. Jones assuring him that the order would be completed within the week. Delay was caused by the unusual weather conditions in the area. He pointed out that there would still be time for planting, and enclosed a pamphlet with full cultural instructions.

4.

```
                              76 Port Street,
                              Tidmarsh,
                              Surrey.

                              17th June, 19..

Craig & Co. Ltd.,
High Street,
Tidmarsh, Surrey.

Dear Sirs,

     Your building foreman called at
this address over two weeks ago to
inspect the garage.  I was then pro-
mised an estimate for the strengthening
of the roof and the resurfacing of the
floor, work requiring prompt attention.

     Since then I have received neither
an estimate nor any indication that you
are prepared to do the work.  I should
like to know if you intend to submit an
estimate;  otherwise I must call in
another firm.

                    Yours faithfully,

                    K. G. Vaughn
```

NOTES FOR THE REPLY:

Mr. Craig regretted that the estimate had not been sent and explained that it was a misunderstanding. He thought that Mr. Vaughn was still deciding whether to strengthen the old garage or have a new one built. He enclosed an estimate for the strengthening and an estimate for replacement, recommending a suitable garage for the site.

5.

```
                              "Slowleigh,"
                              Quince Road,
                              Purview.

                         10th June, 19..

The Borough Surveyor,
Purview Borough Council,
Council Offices, Purview.

Dear Sir,

     As a resident in Quince Road I
regularly use the short cut to Purview
Station through the open space between
numbers 71 and 73.  This is reasonable
during summer and dry weather, but for
a great part of the year the space is
overgrown with nettles, and in wet
weather the path becomes a quagmire.

     I understand that the space will
eventually become a permanent right of
way;  if this is so cannot something be
done to clear the site and make some
temporary surface.

          Yours faithfully,

             K D. Jones
```

NOTES FOR THE REPLY:

The Borough Surveyor informed Mr. Jones that the Council had for some time considered making a right of way but that road repairs had taken priority. Renewal of the building programme had raised the question of building there, but a final decision had not been made. He pointed out another 'short cut' which could be used. The matter would be discussed at the next council meeting.

6.

Oakleaf Cottage,
Corston,
Miltshire.
15th August, 19..

The Town Clerk,
Thurston Borough Council,
Thurston, Miltshire.

Dear Sir,
    We hope to stage a West Miltshire Drama Festival this year and such has been the initial support that I have been asked to enquire whether the Thurston Town Hall will be available for the inaugural Festival during the second or third week in November.
    Although the Festival will not be too ambitious a venture, there will be some complicated backstage work, and I should like to confirm that the Town Hall amenities are suitable.

Yours faithfully,

Grace Armitage

Secretary,

West Miltshire Drama Festival Committee

NOTES FOR THE REPLY:

The Town Clerk informed Miss Armitage that the Hall was available and he described the amenities provided. He considered that they would be suitable for the Festival. He expressed pleasure that the Festival was to be held in Thurston and commented upon the chances of its success.

7.

Tickwell College,
Morton Manor,
Vorlshire.
17th September, 19..

The Manager,
Stantforth Hotel,
Wickworth, Vorlshire.

Dear Sir,
        The Staff Association of this College has decided to hold the annual Dinner Dance this year in Wickworth, a departure from previous years when the function has been held in the college hall.
        I am told that suitable accommodation is available at the Stantforth Hotel, several members of staff having commented upon the excellence of your cuisine. Will you please confirm that you cater for such functions and send details of charges and services.
        If the date is available I should like to make a provisional booking for Saturday, 9th December, from 6.30 p.m. to midnight.

Yours faithfully,
P. B. Coker

Secretary,
Staff Association

NOTES FOR THE REPLY:

The Manager wrote to Mr. Coker regretting that the date mentioned was not available, but that the previous Saturday, the 2nd December, had not been booked. He gave details of the banquet accommodation, cos^t of meals, services, etc., and advised an early reply.

8.
```
                              Houseboat "Windflow,"
                              Riverside Road,
                              Korsten.

                              12th April, 19..

Asken & Co.,
Yacht Suppliers,
Belmont Street,
Melcaster.

Dear Sirs,

        You recently sent me a small con-
signment of ship's crockery and cut-
lery.   In transit by rail several items
of crockery - two cups, four saucers,
and three tea plates - were damaged.

        The crockery was of a pale pink
shade and in a design which I was
particularly eager to have.   I hope
that you will send replacements for the
broken items.

                    Yours faithfully,

                      G. Winborne
```

NOTES FOR THE REPLY:

Mr. E. Asken told his Secretary to inform Mr. Winborne that he regretted the breakage and would claim from the railway. Replacement of broken items was difficult as the set had been specially made and matching would not be easy. He asked whether Mr. Winborne would consider another colour. If so, the original set could be replaced.

9.

WHIZZO SOAP CO. LTD

SLOUGH,
BUCKS.

5th June, 19..

Pole & Sons Ltd.,
Advertising House,
Warwick Street, S.W.10.

Dear Sirs,

With reference to the recent advertising campaign for our new product, I must inform you that the latest sales returns show little increase. Despite intensive competition in the soap and detergent market, other manufacturers have been making substantial profits.

In view of the expense involved in the campaign we should appreciate your observations and suggested reasons for the lack of public response.

Yours faithfully,

B. Rolfe

Managing Director

NOTES FOR THE REPLY:

Mr. Pole told his Secretary to inform the soap company that the campaign had been carefully planned to precede the advertisements issued by rival companies. Unfortunately, a sudden price-slashing in the trade had meant altering the posters thereby losing the vital initial advantage. He suggested a meeting to discuss further policy.

10. The following advertisement appeared in the "Daily News" for 13th October, 19..:

> Shorthand-typist required for shipping office in the City. Work involves report-writing and knowledge of a foreign language. Some experience abroad an advantage. Write stating experience and salary required to Box 432D.

NOTES FOR THE REPLY:

Miss R. Smith writes an application giving details of her education and qualifications. She makes special mention of distinctions in shorthand speed and of experience in report writing gained with a firm of exporters. Speaks and writes French fluently, with working knowledge of two other languages.

I. Additional Letter-writing Exercises

1. *Ordering by Letter*

(a) Write as a retail confectioner to your wholesaler ordering a month's supply.

(b) As secretary of a social club, order from a local printer posters, handbills, etc., for a Christmas Charity.

(c) Your office is short of typing and other stationery, but the quarterly requisition is not due. Order a temporary stock from your supplier.

(d) Your new office will need a small stock of useful reference books. Write a letter ordering these from the bookseller.

(e) Write on behalf of an engineering company to a supplier of heavy machinery. Request servicing of certain machines, and arrange for collection and temporary replacements.

(f) Your firm, manufacturers of biscuits, intends to exhibit at a Food Fair. Write to an advertising agency, asking for stand and display design.

(*g*) Your office is to be improved by the installation of modern equipment. Write a letter to the suppliers of office equipment ordering the items you require.

(*h*) Your employer is going on a business trip to Rome. As secretary, write to a travel agency, making arrangements and giving details of special requirements—business stops, special car service in Rome, etc.

2. *Letters of Enquiry and Complaint*

(*a*) You have lost your portable typewriter on a suburban train. Write to the Railway Lost Property Office, giving details.

(*b*) You have arranged with a builder to have your house decorated. The foreman has inspected the property but several weeks have elapsed without your receiving a letter or an estimate. Write a suitable letter to the builder.

(*c*) For several weeks a noisy machine in a factory near your house has been operated late into the evening. This has caused some distress and inconvenience. Write to the factory, asking for some action to be taken.

(*d*) As manageress of an exclusive dress shop, complain to a couturier about errors in the delivery of certain exclusive model dresses.

(*e*) Write a letter to the firm supplying stationery to your office, complaining about deterioration in the quality of certain items in their last consignment.

(*f*) As secretary of a social club, write to the local council asking for certain facilities to be made available.

3. *Answers to Enquiries*

(*a*) As an official of a borough council reply to a letter of enquiry from a prospective resident. Give information about local amenities.

(*b*) A customer has written to your firm of packers asking for information about the exporting of small household utensils. Reply, suggesting crates to be used—weight, durability, etc., and informing him of transport methods.

(*c*) Write on behalf of a firm of film distributors to a cinema manager who has asked for advance information about films. Give details of future plans and explain the impending introduction of a new cinematic technique.

(d) In reply to a query from a large commercial organization, the Head Office of a chain of hotels gives details of an arrangement for special terms for commercial travellers. Compose this letter.

(e) As landlord of a block of flats, reply to a tenant's enquiry about the need for rules such as "No washing on Sunday," etc.

(f) As secretary to a famous film star, answer a letter from a firm of toothpaste manufacturers asking the star to advertise their product. Explain to the firm that your employer is unable to take on such work, and give her reasons.

(g) Compose a circular letter which is to be sent by a museum to schools in the area, answering a general enquiry about visits and conducted tours.

(h) In answer to a customer's enquiry, your firm of wholesalers gives details of Christmas novelties to be available in the autumn. You suggest suitable 'lines' for that particular customer's shop.

4. *Letters demanding Tact*

(a) As landlord of a row of terraced houses, write to one of your tenants about whom you have received several complaints from neighbours. Inform him that he should keep his dog under control.

(b) Write as a bank manager to one of your clients, asking him to settle his overdraft.

(c) A shoe retailer whom you supply is reported to be overcharging for your goods. Write a suitable letter.

(d) Your publishing firm has received a mediocre manuscript for consideration, and you are not prepared to publish it. Write to the author informing him that the MS cannot be accepted.

(e) As manager of a laundry you have received a letter of complaint from a customer about damaged clothing. The laundered items were torn by cuff-links in a shirt. Write a suitable letter.

(f) As secretary of a tennis club you are asked by the

committee to inform an applicant for membership that he cannot be accepted. The committee have agreed that his standard of play is not high enough.

(g) An employee of your firm has, after long and loyal service, reached retiring age, but has obviously no wish to give up his work. The firm's policy is one of compulsory retirement. As managing director write a careful letter to that employee.

(h) You are in charge of the claims section of an insurance company. Write a letter to a claimant, explaining that you cannot settle his claim as there has been obvious negligence.

5. *Letters of Apology*

(a) From the furniture department of a large store to a customer who complains that he has not received the dining-room suite he ordered. Owing to slight marking the suite has to be replaced, but the customer has not been informed of this.

(b) Reply to a telephone message that you have not stated whether you will be able to preside at a certain function in a few days time. A letter was sent to you earlier about this, but was not answered. You wish to accept the invitation.

(c) From a wholesaler to a customer, apologizing for delivery of the wrong consignment and arranging for prompt replacement.

(d) From a manufacturer to a customer, apologizing for non-delivery of a large order after a definite delivery date had been fixed. Explain that the order has been sent and that the delay was because of a shortage of raw materials.

(e) From the editor of a provincial newspaper to one of the local councillors, apologizing for an unfortunate article, concerning the councillor, which was published in the previous issue.

6. *Circular Letters*

(a) A letter from the Headmaster of a school to the parents, setting out the events for the winter term.

(b) From a charitable organization appealing for subscriptions in aid of a specific cause.

(c) From a newly-opened grocer's shop to prospective customers in the area.

(*d*) From a garage with a large stock of new cars, trying to increase sales by an appeal to owners of old cars to trade in their vehicles.

(*e*) From a local ironmonger, during late winter, offering a discount before a certain date to customers bringing mowers, shears, etc., for sharpening and adjustment.

(*f*) From a sports outfitter, at the onset of the cricket and tennis season, to officials and members of local clubs.

(*g*) From a firm manufacturing and distributing a new detergent, to the householders in several districts, promoting sales by means of discount vouchers. (Try to avoid the well-worn phraseology.)

(*h*) From an examining body to its registered students, notifying them of changes in the syllabus.

(*i*) From the Secretary of a Society, giving notice of a meeting and setting out the agenda.

(*j*) From the local Electricity Showrooms, giving details of a new popular-size washing-up machine.

(*k*) From a new laundry, giving details of a novel door-to-door service.

(*l*) From the local Water Board, giving notice of a temporary interruption of the supply and explaining the reason.

(*m*) From a firm to its customers, giving notice of a change of premises.

(*n*) From a Book Club to members of the general public, trying to gain new subscribers.

J. Composition of a Series of Letters

In each of the following exercises outline notes are given for a series of letters. You are asked to expand those notes into a business-like correspondence between the people concerned. Alternatively, the notes can be used for shorthand practice and expansion into typewritten form.

1. On the 14th May, G. B. Rees of 13 Highfield Road, Barking, writes to the Newfab Upholsterers, West Road, Byfleet, asking for an estimate for re-covering of dining-room chairs. He gives the number and an idea of material required.

On the 19th May, after an inspection, Newfab Upholsterers

quote a price for re-covering in one of a series of fabrics, patterns of which they enclose.

On the 21st May, Mr. Rees chooses a pattern and asks for the work to be done by a certain time.

2. On the 20th November, a retail grocer, T. A. Grant of High Street, Burton, writes to the Cellophane Wrapper Co., Horden, Middlesex, explaining that he is starting a self-service branch and enquiring about suitable wrappings for certain goods.

On the 23rd November, the Wrapper Co. replies with full particulars together with prices and discount arrangements. The company offers to send a representative.

On the 25th November, Mr. Grant, pleased with the information, asks for the representative to call and gives suitable dates and times.

3. On the 10th September, Miss P. Coombs, Hon. Sec., Bransome Literary Society, Oak Cottage, Bransome, writes to Professor B. Smith, West Holly, Birbridge, asking if he will give a short series of lectures to the Society during the winter. She suggests a programme and a general topic.

On the 13th September, the professor agrees to give the lectures, but suggests amendments to the scheme. He gives alternatives and his reasons for the change. He finds the dates suitable but says that a later starting-time would make his journey easier.

On the 16th September, Miss Coombs agrees to the changes and informs the professor that she will make the necessary alterations to the times. She submits an amended draft prospectus for the series.

4. On the 14th December, the Patio Wine Co., 12 Bath Street, Lincoln, inform The Wine Shop, High Street, Grantham, that a delivery is being made of certain Christmas wines, but that some of the wines ordered are not available. Alternatives are suggested.

On the 18th December, The Wine Shop acknowledges the delivery and agrees to certain alternatives in the order. In view of the nearness of Christmas, the manager asks for prompt delivery of the substitutes.

On the 20th December, the Wine Company informs their customer of special arrangements made for direct delivery.

5. On the 11th April, J. R. Browne, 15 Wall Road, Crayton, writes to the Hantley Insurance Co., Lessing Road, Hantley, asking about life insurance and expressing an interest in an endowment policy.

On the 13th April, the Insurance Company explains that there are two forms of endowment insurance—with or without bonus. Premiums depend upon age and the result of a medical examination. A prospectus is enclosed.

On the 16th April, Mr. Browne returns the proposal form detached from the prospectus. He has completed the form for an endowment policy with bonus and asks for a medical examination to be arranged as soon as possible.

SECTION IV

PRÉCIS-WRITING

A. Précis-writing
B. Précis of a Series of Letters

A. Précis-writing

Précis work is perhaps the most searching test of a person's ability in English, exercising three important techniques:

(*a*) Comprehension of the written word,
(*b*) Selection of what is important and relevant,
(*c*) Clear and concise written expression.

It is a process of analysis without the physical aid of test-tubes and reagents, and there are no 'cast-iron' formulae. The ability to grasp the meaning of the original passage and then to select the important ideas comes from constant reading and practice; there is no catchpenny method of overcoming this, although a knowledge of English composition will help. If the writer of the passage uses, as he should, a plan, it will be apparent in his work.

The following method is recommended as a practical approach and as a deterrent to the dangerous 'line-by-line' method to which so many students succumb at the prospect of difficulty. Some of the steps can be omitted as proficiency increases.

(*a*) Read the passage carefully (several times if necessary) to ensure complete understanding.

(*b*) Read again, underlining or making notes of the main points. If the passage is well-paragraphed, make full use of topic sentences as a guide to the relevant ideas. Omit unimportant details. Give conclusions and definite opinions if they occur in the original, but omit arguments, illustrations, and examples, unless the passage is itself an argument leading to a conclusion, when the steps must be shown.

(*c*) Make brief notes of these main points *in your own words*. This is when, having reached something approaching the writer's original plan, you must re-think the passage, expressing it *within your own vocabulary range*.

(*d*) Put the original passage aside and make a rough summary from your own notes. Use simple, clear, and straightforward language, free from figurative and involved expression. Take great care to preserve the connexion of ideas; it is not good enough to have all the main points set down in a disjointed manner.

(*e*) Count the number of words and make any additions or alterations.

(*f*) Compare your draft précis with the original to make sure that there are no omissions.

(*g*) Select a suitable title.

(*h*) Write a fair copy.

(*i*) Make sure that there are no errors of grammar, punctuation, or spelling.

(*j*) Write the number of words (usually excluding the title) at the end of your finished précis.

N.B. Where the original passage is in direct speech it should be changed to reported speech—third person, past tense. Do not overlook the alteration of such words as *to-day*, *this*, *last*, etc.

1. Make a summary of the following passage in about 100–110 words and supply a suitable heading.

A good workman is always assiduous in caring for his tools. It is, therefore, only reasonable that anyone who aspires to be considered a competent typist should take pains to keep in good order so complicated and expensive a tool as her machine. The benefit of such careful treatment is two-fold: the work done on a machine which is clean, in correct alignment, free from friction in all the many moving parts, will look neater and be produced with greater ease, and it will, moreover, be done with much less effort; the machine itself will last longer without any necessity of servicing by the makers, other than a periodic overhaul every few years.

It cannot be too strongly emphasized that, although the regular maintenance is the business of the operator, it is most undesirable that any mechanical defect which may make itself apparent should be tinkered with by inexpert hands. Such a procedure will inevitably lead to straining of some vital part, thus increasing the original defect and in all probability leading to others still more serious.

This regular maintenance is simple and effective—if done with regularity. Cleanliness and oiling are required. The machine should always be covered when not in use, and at the end of each day any accumulation of dust should be removed by means of a soft cloth for those parts easily accessible and a long-handled brush for the interior of the machine.

Oiling is almost as simple. A fine oil especially made for the purpose should be used, and used judiciously. A small camel-hair brush can be used for oiling joints and any point of friction, and individual type-bar bearings should be oiled about twice a year. For these the eye of a darning-needle dipped in oil will take up sufficient for each bearing. Should a squeaking or grating noise become apparent the source must be located and treated, not the whole machine haphazard.

[R.S.A. S.T.C. Stage II Inter.]

2. Your employer has asked you to summarize the following report. Do so as briefly as possible but omit nothing of importance. Do not exceed 100 words.

I do not wish to finish without voicing my appreciation of the Staff, and for what they have done during most difficult times. The Staff at our Works deserve special mention. During this year we have had two setbacks, one connected with enemy action, the other not. Each in its way has thrown very great strain on our Staff, and both have shown what wonderful power and ability lie within the British character.

It is therefore with more confidence that we recommend that you should transfer the sum of £10,000 to the Staff Fund. This not only increases the total of the Pension Fund and allows for the bonus to Staff which we paid last year, but also provides a balance for the current year which will help considerably and may allow both these benefits to continue on a sound basis for another year. I know that the Managers of the various sections will be able to find means of showing to the Staff the gratitude of the Shareholders, and the thanks of Directors and Shareholders.

Again we are delayed by the mails from overseas in making up and publishing the final figures. You will see that in one case we have acted on cabled figures, and not on the usual accounts received by mail. At any rate, this delay has the advantage that any statement about future prospects can be based as to part on the experience of over five months' trade. That part remains very bright, both in Great Britain and in the rest of the English-speaking world. The other part—the future—is also very hopeful. The risk of the unexpected is greater in Great Britain than overseas, but we can only hope that we may be allowed to continue with the least possible disturbance to our work in what is a most important aspect of man's activities, particularly under present-day war conditions.

[R.S.A. S.T.C. Stage II Inter.]

3. Summarize the following discussion in not more than *about* 75 words. Do not refer to the members of the Committee by name.

CHAIRMAN: I think that there is nothing more to say on that subject, so we will now consider Item 5 on the Agenda—the Christmas bonus. First, I will ask the Treasurer for his ideas on the subject.

TREASURER: For the benefit of members who were not on the Committee last year, I had better explain how the payment of the bonus has been made in the past. It has long been our custom to make a present to each of the nine members of the Club Staff at Christmas. It has been calculated as a percentage of each employee's salary, one per cent of the yearly salary. Last year that amounted to £22 10s. 0d. I propose that the same payments be made again this year.

MR ABBOTT: Mr Chairman, could we be told the details of these payments? I suppose all these people don't get the same sum.

CHAIRMAN: Mr Brown, will you let us hear these details?

TREASURER: Certainly, Mr Chairman. Porter £3; Head Waiter, £3; Second Waiter, £2 10s. 0d.; Housekeeper, £5; Cook, £4; two Kitchenmaids, £2 10s. 0d. each; two Chambermaids, £2 10s. 0d.

CHAIRMAN: Thank you. Is that what you wanted to know, Mr Abbott?

MR ABBOTT: Yes. But I think it is a pity that these distinctions are made. Surely it would be better to give them all the same amount. After all, we are not paying them a bit extra exactly. We're giving them Christmas presents.

MR COTMAN: Mr Chairman, I agree with the last speaker. I think they all ought to have the same amount.

SECRETARY: Mr Chairman, may I make a remark here?

CHAIRMAN: Certainly, Mr Dolland.

SECRETARY: It would be a little awkward to cut down the amounts we have always given to Miss Fenton and Mrs Gedge. They have been with us a number of years. I think they would feel hurt.

MR ABBOTT: Then could we fix it on a calculation of how long they have been with us.

CHAIRMAN: What do the rest of the Committee feel about this?

MR LYWOOD: I don't suppose that would work out. I imagine that the staff didn't all come at the same time. I should think the porter has been here longer than any of the others.

MR HAMMOND: Couldn't we give them something else—cigarettes or something? Must it be money?

CHAIRMAN: Could we be sure of what they wanted? I know the Head Waiter doesn't smoke. Asthma!

MR LYWOOD: I think we had better do as we have done in previous years. I should like to propose that the Christmas bonuses be allocated in the usual way.

CHAIRMAN: Thank you. Will some one second that proposal? Thank you Mr Brown. Those in favour? Those against? The proposal is carried.

[R.S.A. S.T.C. Part II Inter.]

4. Make a summary of the following passage in about 100–110 words and supply a suitable heading.

We have published a "Warning to Authors and Others" every year for many years past, but every year we continue to receive letters from writers and others so determined to see their work in print that they have been persuaded to pay for its publication themselves. May we emphasize again that an author or an artist should never pay for publication except under the two special circumstances noted below: some magazines of a specialist nature are not published for commercial profit and it may be considered an honour to have work published in them. It should be apparent which journals come into this class. If a book is of an extremely specialized nature and if the market for the book is very limited, it is not unusual for some contribution to be made towards the cost of publication. It must be emphasized, however, that the number of such books is extremely small and at least 99 per cent of books published each year do not come within this category. Many distressing cases are brought to our notice where authors have contributed to the cost of publication of works of a general nature, and we do not apologize therefore for repeating the warning.

Never pay for publication, whether it is for a book, an article, a piece of music, or for setting a lyric to music. If a work is worth publishing, sooner or later a publisher will recognize its merits and be prepared to publish it at his own expense. Every one with literary or artistic work to sell is advised to proceed with caution before submitting work to a firm about which he knows little or nothing. A precautionary step which few people take is to send a preliminary letter. If a magazine or firm is overstocked they will say so. If no reply is received nothing is lost except a little time. Some writers seeking publication for a book send a duplicated letter of enquiry. It may be said that this type of approach is not one calculated to stimulate a publisher's curiosity. A writer would be advised to select his publisher with discrimination and to approach him with an individual letter.

[From Preface to *Writer's and Artist's Year Book*, 1954]

5. Condense the following speech into a paragraph of about 150 words suitable for publication in a newspaper. Supply a headline of not more than *six* words.

Ladies and Gentlemen, as your Chairman has already explained to you, this question of the Flower Show must be decided at this meeting. Those of you who were at the Annual Meeting last year will no doubt remember that there was a long discussion about it then, but for the benefit of those who were not at that meeting it would perhaps be helpful if I as Secretary were to run over a few points. It has long been the custom of this Horticultural Society to hold a flower show every year. At one time it was well supported, but of recent years there has been a decided falling-off in the number of entries and in the attendance at the Show itself. Two years ago we did just succeed in meeting our expenses but last year the Show resulted in a loss. Fortunately we had some money in hand which enabled us to cover that loss, but our balance at the moment is so small—just over £12 as a matter of fact—that the Committee does not feel justified in holding a show at all unless some different arrangements are made. I know we were unfortunate last year in our weather. The day of the Show was cold and wet, as I expect you remember, but that was no excuse for the small number of entries. The entry forms have to be in several weeks before the Show actually takes place, and would-be exhibitors, though we all know they are clever gardeners, are not equally clever as weather prophets.

The point is this—do the people of Moreton Green really want to support it? That is what the Committee must know. We cannot go forward with our arrangements for this year's Show on our usual scale and risk another fiasco. Various suggestions were put forward at our Committee meeting last week, and the conclusion we came to was that we had better be less ambitious this year. Instead of going to the expense of putting up a marquee in Mr Foljambe's paddock we are proposing to hold the Show in the Church Hall, which the Vicar is prepared to let us have on the Saturday before Bank Holiday, August 1st, and I am sure we are all very grateful for his kind offer. So will you all please arrange not to be away on holiday on that day and do your best to make this year's Flower Show a real success? The entry forms are available now and the Assistant Secretary will let you have them as you go out. The rest is up to you Ladies and Gentlemen. If you do your part, the Show will go well and we can look forward to a show every year, just as good as those we held in the past.

[R.S.A. S.T.C. Stage II Inter.]

6. Rewrite the following letter—retaining the letter form—expressing the facts as concisely as possible. Reduce to about 140 words.

St Anne's College,
Camford.
13th July, 1953

Dear Miss Anderton,

Thank you for your letter of July 10th asking me to give some talks to the Camford Girls' Club on the evenings of Oct. 5 and 19 and Nov. 2 and 16 this autumn.

I regret that I am not sure that I shall be free on every one of these evenings. I shall be available on Oct. 5 and Nov. 2; but on Oct. 19 I shall be engaged and possibly on Nov. 16 also. I can, however, come on Nov. 23 and Dec. 7.

I understand that the sort of talk you have in mind is something in the nature of a course on some literary or historical subject. I have given a number of such courses to groups of young people like the members of your Club and have found them popular with my audiences. But in this case I am not sure that such an arrangement would be a good one, as the length of time which must elapse between the separate talks might lead to a slackening of interest in the subject-matter. In the circumstances, it might be better to have four talks, each of which would be complete in itself but all of them having some connexion.

For example, if you preferred to have talks on literary subjects only, I could begin on Oct. 5 with "The Pleasures of Reading." This makes a good introduction to a literary course. I point out, first, what one may expect to gain from reading both the classics and the best of the moderns, in fiction and non-fiction. Then I explain how one may obtain books from local libraries and from County and Students' libraries. This could be followed by three talks on any particular writer or period about which your members might like to hear in more detail.

If you thought that a historical series would be more popular, the first talk could be "The History of Camford," a subject on which many inhabitants of our town are surprisingly ignorant. That could be followed by a visit, on the next evening when I come to the Club, to the Camford Museum. As I am one of the Trustees of the Museum I should be able to show you some of the treasures which are not usually on show to the public, some because they are too valuable or fragile, others because they are too large to be staged in the public rooms. As in the case of the literary talks, I could on the other two evenings take as my subjects anything in which your members had a particular interest.

I should be glad if you would let me know which of these suggestions appeals more to you.

Yours very truly,

ALLEN BOWLES

[R.S.A. S.T.C. Stage II Inter.]

7. Write a précis in 160 words of the following passage and supply a suitable title.

The old and established arts, whether they be crafts or fine arts, have evolved in the course of time a tradition which governs their various forms and the legitimate and illegitimate use of their various mediums—words, paint and canvas, wood and stone, the variety of musical sounds. The long and elaborate history of these arts is the story of the young artists in revolt against the tradition established by their elders and predecessors, from which rebellion further tradition is developed to add to that already practised.

The success of an artist depends largely on his facility in the medium he has chosen. This is partly native to him, partly acquired by practice and experiment. It also depends largely on whether he has sufficient valuable human experience in him which demands expression, and so forces him to undertake the labour of practice and experiment in his medium in order that he can convey this experience satisfactorily to his fellows. To use another language of criticism, he must be not only inspired but also in technique a master of his art.

Tradition, which has much to be said against it when it overwhelms the new vitality of a growing artist, has this advantage, that it gives dignity to the creator and guidance in his first attempts to pursue his art. So long as he is not subjugated by it, he may largely succeed through its example.

To the person who can discern the work of a good artist, a great part of the satisfaction is derived from "the sense of difficulty overcome." Enterprising human beings like to set themselves problems and achieve the solution with the minimum of time and effort: the less enterprising enjoy watching the others. This is as true of a crowd at a football match as of a professor enjoying a poem by Horace. The difference lies only in the quality of human skill and emotion involved.

All works of art, therefore, are successful because of, not in spite of, the limitations their form imposes on them. A painter must achieve vitality and depth through the colour and composition of his picture, which is none the less two-dimensional and static; the composer must communicate a sense of complex human experience, without the assistance of words and pictures, by the encompassed dynamic of sound; the poet must solve an enigma of experience within the sparse framework of a sonnet; a dramatist must achieve his purpose on the bare boards of a stage within the time an audience will pay to sit his drama out. The film director must achieve his aim by means of a succession of flat though mobile pictures, photographed on celluloid and joined together in long sequence. In all these arts the sense of triumph lies not merely in the humanity of the subject or the story, but also in the skill with which the artist moves freely within his self-imposed limits.

[From *Film*, by Roger Manvell]

8. At the Annual General Meeting of Amalgamated Processes Ltd, the Chairman delivered the Annual report. Make a summary of the report in about 140–150 words and supply a suitable heading.

In presenting the Balance Sheet for the year 1952 your directors are pleased to be able to report for the second year in succession a marked increase in the net profits and a general improvement in turnover and they are the more pleased to be able to do so as this has resulted from their steady pursuance of the policy of maintaining equipment at the very highest level of efficiency and replacing at the earliest possible moment all equipment the continuing efficiency of which they had any cause to doubt. An examination of the Balance Sheet before you will show that the figures for maintenance and replacement are high. That your directors admit, but they submit to you that there is no cause for alarm or despondency, since these figures are balanced by others, even higher than usual, on the other side.

You are aware, of course, that overseas trading is still very difficult. Many of our former markets, for reasons with which you are only too painfully familiar, remain almost or wholly closed to us. Nevertheless I feel that this state of affairs need cause no undue concern. There are already signs—at the moment too slight to be termed more than fairly encouraging— which can be interpreted by those in close contact with the general trend of trade as at least not discouraging, and you may rest assured that your directors are not neglecting any opportunity to take advantage of every opening that can be discerned. As and when such openings present themselves they will be seized without any delay.

Meanwhile every advantage has been taken of the increasing opportunities in the home market. Our business in this country has been 60 per cent of our total business during the whole of the year, an increase of 8 per cent on last year's figures. No slackening of effort will be allowed to hamper our success in this market for the ensuing twelve months.

Your directors recommend a dividend of 12 per cent as against the previous dividend of 10 per cent and they feel that this will in no way impair the Company's resources.

He would be a bold man who in these difficult days would hazard a detailed prophecy as to the future but I feel justified in predicting no great drop in our turnover. Your directors keep ever in mind the problem before them and I think you may indulge in at least a modest hope of business being better still next year.

The Report and Balance Sheet were then adopted.

[R.S.A. S.T.C. Stage III Adv.]

9. Write a précis of the following passage in 160 words and provide a suitable title.

Before we can form an adequate mental picture of the way in which an eye works, we must consider two inventions which, probably unknowingly, man has modelled on certain structures in the eye. One of them, the convex lens, is of great antiquity, and probably antedates any knowledge of the structure of the eye. The other, the photo electric selenium cell, is a recent discovery, and its analogy to certain of the mechanisms of sight was well perceived from the beginning, as its popular name, the "electric eye," shows.

To start with the convex lens. This is to-day a piece of glass ground and polished so that its surfaces are not parallel to each other, but are curved, each surface being a portion of a sphere. In other words, the lens is thicker in the middle than at the edges and is evenly curved. The use of such lenses to magnify objects and to set fire to objects by concentrating the light and heat of the sun on them was well known to the Chinese and the Graeco-Roman worlds centuries ago. They were then made of rock crystal and other natural transparent materials, and the memory of that period (which extended to comparatively modern times) still lingers in the term "pebbles" used for spectacle lenses by old countrymen, and "burning glass" used by children for hand magnifying lenses.

Light travels in straight lines in air until it meets a transparent surface of different density—e.g., a surface of water or of glass. It is then deflected or bent at this surface and continues on in a straight line in the medium (water or glass) at an angle to its original path. This phenomenon, called refraction, is well known, though we do not think much about it. No one is surprised that a straight stick looks bent when partly under water, or that a water flea looks as big as a rabbit when seen through a microscope. Both these appearances depend on this property which transparent materials possess of altering the direction of rays of light passing through them. Indeed, much of the background of our modern life depends on the use of such arrangements (called lenses) to bend rays of light in such a way as to form pictures, which we then use for various purposes of pleasure, instruction, and destruction. Cameras, microscopes, telescopes, cinemas, magic lanterns, reading spectacles, bomb-sights, periscopes are all possible because of this property of refraction and because, if the surface of the refracting substance is evenly curved and is convex, the parallel rays of light entering it will all approach each other and will, when they leave it again, form a small sharp picture of the object from which they came. The distance of this picture (or image) from the lens will depend on its curve. The more highly curved the lens is, the nearer the picture will be to it. This distance is called the focal length of the lens.

[From *The Science of Seeing*, by Ida Mann
and A. Pirie]

10. Make a précis of the following passage in not more than 160 words and compose a suitable title.

In almost all its manifestations, however, war indicates a throw-back to an infantile psychical pattern on the part of people who can no longer stand the exacting strain of life in groups, with all the necessities for compromise, give-and-take, live-and-let-live, understanding and sympathy, that such life demands, and with all the complexities of adjustment involved. They seek by the knife and the gun to unravel the social knot. But whereas national wars to-day are essentially collective competitions in which the battlefield takes the place of the market, the ability of war to command the loyalty and interests of the entire underlying population rests partly upon its peculiar psychological reactions: it provides an outlet and an emotional release. "Art degraded, imagination denied," as Blake says, "war governed the nations."

For war is the supreme drama of completely mechanized society; and it has an element of advantage that puts it high above the other preparatory forms of mass-sport in which the attitudes of war are mimicked: war is real, while in all other mass-sports there is an element of make-believe: apart from the excitements of the game and the gains and losses from gambling, it does not really matter who is victorious. In war, there is no doubt as to the reality: success may bring the reward of death just as surely as failure, and it may bring it to the remotest spectator as well as to the gladiators in the centre of the vast arena of nations.

But war, for those actually engaged in combat, likewise brings a release from the sordid motives of profit-making and self-seeking that govern the prevailing forms of business enterprise, including sport: the action has the significance of high drama. And while warfare is one of the principal sources of mechanism, and its drill and regimentation are the very pattern of old-style industrial effort, it provides, far more than the sport-field, the necessary compensations to this routine. The preparation of the soldier, the parade, the smartness and polish of the equipment and uniform, the precise movement of large bodies of men, the blare of bugle, the punctuation of drums, the rhythm of the march, and then, in actual battle itself, the final explosion of effort in the bombardment and the charge, lend an aesthetic and moral grandeur to the whole performance. The death or maiming of the body gives the drama the element of a tragic sacrifice, like that which underlies so many primitive religious rituals: the effort is sanctified and intensified by the scale of the holocaust.

E

For peoples that have lost the values of culture and can no longer respond with interest or understanding to the symbols of culture, the abandonment of the whole process, and the reversion to crude faiths and non-rational dogmas are powerfully abetted by the process of war. If no enemy really existed, it would be necessary to create him, in order to further this development.

[From *Technics and Civilization*, by Lewis Mumford]

B. Précis of a Series of Letters

(*a*) Construct a title which should read:

A summary of the correspondence between . . . .

. . . . . . of . . . ., and . . . . of

. . . ., concerning . . . .

(*b*) Read the letters carefully and make rough notes of their main points, setting these notes under the appropriate letter dates.

(*c*) From the notes, construct a précis in indirect speech, including the dates but discarding the letter form.

(*d*) Count the number of words and make any necessary additions or alterations.

(*e*) Make your fair copy and write the number of words at the end.

In the following exercises you are asked to write a summary of each set of three letters in about 75 words (not including the heading). For Exercises 7, 8, 9, and 10 the summary should be about 100 words in length.

I.

> 18 Landsdowne Road,
> Purview,
> Stenshire.
>
> 12th May, 19..

The Manager,
Benbow Garage,
High Street,
Sleightly, Stenshire.

Dear Sir,

I understand that the car I have just bought from your garage - a $2\frac{1}{2}$ litre Stanton Special - has now been overhauled and is in good running order.

There are, however, two items which I had overlooked and which could best be dealt with at this stage. I think that some form of undersealing would give greater protection, and the replacement of the present cylinder head by a special aluminium type would give improved performance.

Will you, please, proceed with these two jobs and inform me when the car is ready for collection.

> Yours faithfully,
>
> *D. B. Yatesworth*

Benbow Garage,
High Street,
Sleightly, Stenshire.

14th May, 19..

D. B. Yatesworth Esq.,
18 Landsdowne Road,
Purview, Stenshire.

Dear Sir,

Thank you for your letter of the 12th May, asking for further work to be done on your Stanton car.

I have given instructions for the car to be undersealed and it should be ready within three days; but I must inform you that there will be an extra charge for cleaning before the rubber coating is applied.

The fitting of an aluminium cylinder head will present no difficulty, but there may be a delay of a week or more before the head can be supplied. It is not, however, vital to the running of your car and you will be able to collect it after the undersealing has been completed.

I shall notify you when the new cylinder head arrives so that you can arrange to bring your car in again.

Yours faithfully,

E P Strange

Manager

18 Landsdowne Road,
Purview,
Stenshire.

15th May, 19..

The Manager,
Benbow Garage,
High Street,
Sleightly, Stenshire.

Dear Sir,

Thank you for your letter of the 14th May and the advice given. Please notify me by telephone when the undersealing has been completed.

There is no urgency for the new cylinder head.

Yours faithfully,

D. B. Yatesworth.

2.

Bates & Forbes Ltd.,
High Street,
Kesby, Herts.

17th July, 19..

The Manager,
The Stanley Milk Company,
Rigby,
Hants.

Dear Sir,

Double-strength Stancreme

Sales of the above product have
been reasonably successful so far this
summer, but many customers have en-
quired about the use and treatment of
the cream. They complain that whipping
is difficult even with the use of an
electric mixer.

We have been unable to give them
any advice and feel that, unless we can
pass some helpful information on to the
customer, sales will be affected. The
addition of gelatine has been suggested, but we find that in practice
this is not effective.

We should be grateful for any
advice you can give.

Yours faithfully,

E. E. Forbes

Sales Manager

The Stanley Milk Company,
Rigby,
Hants.

19th July, 19..

The Sales Manager,
Bates & Forbes Ltd.,
High Street,
Kesby, Herts.

Dear Sir,

Double-strength Stancreme

With reference to your letter of
the 17th July, enquiring about the
whipping of our synthetic cream, I am
sorry that you have experienced trouble
with this new product. Our labora-
tories have, however, provided the following information which you can safely
pass on to your customers.

The cream must be chilled before
whipping and the best method is to
stand the tin in a refrigerator or
freezing box for 24 hours. This will
separate the whey, leaving a thicker
cream which can be whipped quite
easily. Gelatine may be added during
this process, but it must first be
mixed with a little hot water.

We are arranging to produce a
small leaflet explaining this method

and will send copies as soon as they
are available.

Yours faithfully,

P. R. Smith

Manager

Bates & Forbes Ltd.,
High Street,
Kesby, Herts.

22nd July, 19..

The Manager,
The Stanley Milk Company,
Rigby, Hants.

Dear Sir,

Double-strength Stancreme

Thank you for your letter of the
19th July, in which you explained the
correct method of whipping your synthetic cream.

We feel sure that this information
will be helpful to customers, especially if the sale of the cream is
accompanied by explanatory leaflets.

You did not mention the quantity
of gelatine to be used, but this will
no doubt be stated in the printed
instructions.

Thank you for your prompt attention to our enquiry.

Yours faithfully,

Q. Q. Forbes

Sales Manager

3.

Park Lodge,
Park Avenue,
Milton.

14th June, 19..

Berowne Watch Co. Ltd.,
High Street,
Milchester.

Dear Sirs,

I am returning under separate cover a watch that I purchased about two years ago. It has given good service since then, but recently became very unreliable and eventually stopped.

Will you please send me an estimate for its repair.

Yours faithfully,

K. Browne

Berowne Watch Co. Ltd.,
High Street,
Milchester.

19th June, 19..

K. Browne Esq.,
Park Lodge,
Park Avenue, Milton.

Dear Sir,

We have safely received the watch mentioned in your letter of the 14th June. The hair spring is broken, and will cost about ten shillings to replace.

During the inspection of the watch, our mechanic discovered that the balance wheel was of the wrong size. It appears that the wrong wheel was fitted in an earlier repair, not materially affecting the action of the watch but preventing really accurate timekeeping. We can, if you wish, fit a new balance wheel for a small charge.

We await your instructions concerning the hair spring and your comments on replacing the balance wheel.

Yours faithfully,

J. Hawkes

Manager

Park Lodge,
Park Avenue,
Milton.

21st June, 19..

Berowne Watch Co. Ltd.,
High Street,
Milchester.

Dear Sirs,

Thank you for your letter of the
19th June. Please proceed with the
repair of my watch.

I was surprised to learn of the
wrong-sized balance wheel, but can now
recall the occasion of the repair, and
must say that I have noticed little
effect. As the watch was not expensive
I do not think it will be necessary to
replace the balance wheel.

Yours faithfully,

K. Browne

4.

Hillside,
Cremorne Road,
Seltham,
Hants.

26th August, 19..

The Manager,
All Britain Touring Coaches,
Winchester.

Dear Sir,

On the 15th August, I travelled by
one of your coaches from Ilfracombe to
Bristol, where I changed into a second
coach leaving for Winchester at 2.15.
I left this coach at Seltham and my
suitcase was then found to be missing.

At Bristol I understood from the
driver that he would see to all the
luggage being transferred from one
coach to the other but he evidently did
not do so.

Will you please let me know if my
suitcase has been sent to your coach
station? It is of brown leatherette,
with leather corners and two locks and
marked with the initials R.D.F.

Yours faithfully,

R. Finch (Mrs)

All Britain Touring Coaches,
Winchester.

28th August, 19..

Mrs R. Finch,
Hillside,
Cremorne Road,
Seltham.

Dear Madam,

Thank you for your letter of the
26th August.

I am pleased to be able to tell
you that your suitcase has been for-
warded from the coach station at
Bristol to our Lost Property Office
here. If it is inconvenient for you to
collect it from this office, I will
arrange to have it sent to you at
Seltham. The coaches for Bristol stop
at Seltham Market Cross at 10.30 and
2.30 each day and the suitcase could be
put off at whichever time you prefer.

I must, however, point out that,
although the drivers of our coaches do
in fact stow passengers' cases in the
luggage compartment, it is the responsibility of the owners to see that this
is done. Your case carried no label of
any kind, and the driver of the coach
has reported to us that he was unable
to discover its owner before the
departure schedule obliged him to leave
Bristol.

Yours faithfully,

S. Abby

Hillside,
Cremorne Road,
Seltham.

29th August, 19..

The Manager,
All Britain Touring Coaches,
Winchester.

Dear Sir,

    I am much obliged to you for your
letter of 28th August. I regret having
put you to so much trouble about my
suitcase, but I had not before travelled by coach and was somewhat
bewildered by the noise and bustle of
the coach station.

    Will you send my case by the
morning coach to-morrow, 30th August,
and I will be at the Market Cross at
10.30 to receive it.

    I should like to express my appre-
ciation of your helpful suggestion to
save me the trouble of collecting it
myself.

Yours faithfully,

R. Finch (Mrs)

[R.S.A. S.T.C. Inter.]

5.

Park Cottage,
Benford.

14th April, 19..

The Forsyte Galleries,
High Street,
Benham.

Dear Sirs,

I understand that you provide a
special advisory service for furnishing
and interior decoration. I have been
considering altering the decor of my
dining room, and would like you to send
some one to see what improvements can
be made. I do not contemplate anything
in the so-called contemporary style.

Yours faithfully,

Agnes Smith (Mrs)

                              The Forsyte Galleries,
                              High Street,
                              Benham.
                                20th April, 19..

Mrs A. Smith,
Park Cottage,
Benford.

Dear Madam,
        With reference to your letter of
the 14th April, and our representative's visit, we have pleasure in
submitting a scheme of furnishing and
decorating for your dining room.
        A dining suite with oval table
will make best use of the space available and will give seating for six.   In
view of the aspect, we suggest a light
wall paint or a pale, small-patterned
paper.   The present light-fitting could
be replaced by an adjustable pendant
lamp with a specially-made shade to
tone with or match the curtain fabrics
which should be of a positive shade and
pattern.   A plain, maroon carpet would
have an effect of warmth and contrast.
        To help in your choice of par-
ticular designs and patterns, we
enclose catalogues and samples of
fabrics which our expert has marked
with appropriate comments.   If you will
select the items you want we shall
submit a detailed estimate.

                    Yours faithfully,

                       P. Forsyte

            for The Forsyte Galleries
Encs. 4.

Park Cottage,
Benford.

23rd April, 19..

The Forsyte Galleries,
High Street,
Benham.

Dear Sirs,

Thank you for your letter and
enclosures of the 20th April. I have
decided upon the following items:

Swedish dining room suite, Catalogue
    No. DB 432.
Hand-blocked wallpaper, Pattern
    No. 47.
Curtain fabric, heavy weight,
    Pattern No. 7.
Wonderweave carpet, 2nd weight,
    maroon.

I should like the pendant lamp-
fitting, but with a contrasting fabric
shade in pink.

Yours faithfully,

Agnes Smith (Mrs)

6.

52 Broadway,
Cheam,
Surrey.

31st May, 19..

Willowby & Wood Ltd.,
Newsagents,
27 High Street,
Cheam, Surrey.

Dear Sirs,

We understand that a special
supplement to "The Times" newspaper is
to be published during July dealing
with the mining industry and mining
machinery, and we shall be glad if you
will let us have twenty copies on the
day of publication.

Please deliver them to the above
address and show the cost of them as a
separate item when you render our
monthly account.

Yours faithfully,

Jackson and Grimsey Ltd.

Willowby & Wood Ltd.,
Newsagents,
27 High Street,
Cheam, Surrey.

1st June, 19..

Jackson & Grimsey Ltd.,
52 Broadway,
Cheam, Surrey.

Dear Sirs,

Thank you for your letter of the
31st May. We have recorded your order
for the special supplement to "The
Times" to be published in July, and you
may expect to receive the twenty copies
on the day of publication.

Yours faithfully,

Willowby & Wood Ltd.

52 Broadway,
Cheam,
Surrey.

8th July, 19..

Willowby & Wood Ltd.,
Newsagents,
27 High Street,
Cheam, Surrey.

Dear Sirs,

On the 31st May we wrote to you ordering twenty copies of "The Times" supplement on mining to be published this month and we had a reply from you dated the 1st June in which you stated that they would be supplied on the day of publication.

We now learn from another source that the supplement in question came out on the 4th July and was supplied to some of our business friends by their newsagents on that day.

Kindly let us know why we have not received the twenty copies which were ordered by us.

Yours faithfully,

Jackson and Grimsey Ltd.

[R.S.A. S.T.C. Stage II Inter.]

N.B. The following exercises are for reduction to 100 words.

7.

J. WHITE & SON LTD.
Publishers

GRANT ROAD,
LONDON, E.C.4.

13th May, 19..

T. Jones Esq.,
Vine Cottage,
Pulton, Berks.

Dear Mr Jones,

"Swift Journey"

Thank you for the half-tone illustrations and the black-and-white
sketches which you recently submitted
in connexion with the above MS.

Most of the black-and-white
sketches will be suitable, but the
detailed sketch of a vertical-take-off
aeroplane would lose its subtle definition in the block-making process. As
the illustration is essential to the
text, I should like a simpler version.

The line sketches will be inserted
in the text where you have indicated,
but the half-tones present a different
problem, their position depending upon
the process of binding. Perhaps you
could give me an initial idea of the
order you would like.

Yours sincerely,

J. White

Managing Editor

Vine Cottage,
Pulton,
Berks.

15th May, 19..

The Managing Editor,
J. White & Son Ltd.,
Grant Road, E.C.4.

Dear Mr White,

<u>"Swift Journey"</u>

Thank you for your letter of the
13th May. I am pleased that you consider the illustrations suitable and
can appreciate the difficulties involved in the black-and-white sketch
you mention.
Fortunately I have a less detailed
line-drawing of the aeroplane and will
send it under separate cover.
I should like the half-tone illustrations to be arranged as near as
possible in the following order:

Chapter 1 - Nos. 1, 2, and 3

Chapter 4 - No. 4

Chapter 9 - Nos. 5 and 6

Chapter 15 - Nos. 7, 8, and 9

Chapter 24 - No. 10

Yours sincerely,

T. Jones

J. WHITE & SON LTD.
Publishers

GRANT ROAD,
LONDON, E.C.4.

19th May, 19..

T. Jones Esq.,
Vine Cottage,
Pulton, Berks.

Dear Mr Jones,

"Swift Journey"

Thank you for your letter of the 15th May, and for the replacement sketch which we received to-day. The new sketch is just what is required and has been sent to the block-makers together with your other drawings.

With reference to your running order for the half-tones, I would point out that it is difficult to spread them through the book in odd groups of one, two, and three. If the plates are in pairs they can be stitched into the book around the signatures. Otherwise they would have to be pasted in - a laborious process and one which gives unsatisfactory results. I suggest, however, that you leave the positioning to me and I shall try to arrange them as near as possible to your suggested order.

Yours sincerely,

B. White.

Managing Editor

8.

15 Rowland Avenue,
London, S.W.2.

19th February, 19..

Messrs Arkwright & Wilkins,
89 High Street,
Cottenham, Essex.

Dear Sirs,

I have seen the house at 72
Sheldon Lane, for which I had from you
the order to view. I am prepared to
buy it at the price asked, £2000, if
the owner will have the necessary
repairs done. There are a number of
slipped tiles in the roof and the bedroom ceiling below is damaged by rain
leaking through. In fact, a good deal
of the plaster has fallen.

If it is more convenient to your
client, I will take over the property
as it stands for £1800.

Yours truly,

Henry Doubleday.

Arkwright & Wilkins,
House & Estate Agents,
89 High Street,
Cottenham, Essex.
23rd February, 19..

H. Doubleday Esq.,
15 Rowland Avenue,
London, S. W. 2.

Dear Sir,

72 Sheldon Lane, Cottenham

In reply to your letter of the 19th February, we wish to state that the damage to the above premises, namely slipped tiles in the roof and fallen plaster from a bedroom ceiling, has been scheduled as War Damage to be made good by the Local Authority.

Our client, Col. Fossett, tells us that the assessment of the claim has been agreed and he holds all the documents relating thereto, which documents are to be handed to the new owner in due course. In consideration of these facts Col. Fossett is not prepared to sell for less than the figure originally mentioned. We think that this price is not excessive, in view of the present scarcity of house property.

As we have had other enquiries about this house, we should be glad to hear from you as soon as possible.

Yours faithfully,

T. F. Wilkins

Arkwright & Wilkins

15 Rowland Avenue,
London, S. W. 2.

25th February, 19..

Messrs Arkwright & Wilkins,
89 High Street,
Cottenham, Essex.

Dear Sirs,

Thank you for your letter of the 23rd February.

As the repair of the War Damage has been arranged for, I shall be pleased to buy the house at 72 Sheldon Lane, Cottenham, at the figure of £2000 (Two Thousand Pounds).

I shall be obliged if you will go ahead with the matter at once. In particular I should like to have the papers relating to the claim for damage, so that I may begin at once what may be the long business of getting the roof seen to.

Yours truly,

Henry Doubleday.

[R.S.A. S.T.C. Adv.]

9.

Oakleigh,
Pints Lane,
Venner.

15th March, 19..

Jones & Sons Ltd.,
Builders,
High Street, Venner.

Dear Sirs,

Plot 10, Venner Park Estate

With reference to the building on the above site, I should like to enquire about the method of heating. You will remember that I require whole-house heating and a fairly even temperature throughout, though I am not concerned about the type of fuel used as long as it requires the minimum of attention.

I have had good reports of the under-floor heating by copper piping, but I understand that the installation and running costs are high.

Yours faithfully,

David Gray.

Jones & Sons, Ltd.,
High Street,
Venner.

18th March, 19..

D. Gray Esq.,
Oakleigh,
Pints Lane, Venner.

Dear Sir,

Plot 10, Venner Park Estate

Thank you for your letter of the
15th March enquiring about the heating
system for the above building project.

There is a wide choice of heating
methods, especially with a new property, and you will be wise to plan carefully before building begins.

The system of copper piping you
mentioned is expensive to install but
can be quite effective. If under-floor
electric heating is used, there is a
special allowance for off-peak use of
electricity which enables the heat to
be built up at night to give warmth to
the house for the ensuing day.

Solid-fuel systems are at present
the cheapest to run and are not expensive to install. The modern coke
boiler is a much cleaner method of
heating than its predecessors and is
simple to operate with its gravity feed
and thermostatic control.

Gas and oil heating-systems are both clean and efficient, the running-costs being roughly between those of solid fuel and electricity. Any of these systems can be linked to radiators or warm-air-ducts.

If you will let us know the particular method in which you are interested, we shall be pleased to give more detailed information.

Yours faithfully,

Jones & Sons Ltd.

K. Jones

Sales Manager

Oakleigh,
Pints Lane,
Venner.

20th March, 19..

The Sales Manager,
Jones & Sons Ltd.,
High Street,
Venner.

Dear Sir,

Plot 10, Venner Park Estate

Thank you for the helpful information in your letter of the 18th March. I think that the under-floor method would be too costly, and I have had second thoughts about the permanence of the piping in the concrete.

You have reassured me about the modern solid-fuel burners, and if, as you say, they are easier to maintain and are less dirty, their economy of operation is an important factor.

Will you, please, send me more details of solid-fuel boilers and a suitable system of radiators bearing in mind the size of the house.

Yours faithfully,

David Gray.

10.

The Plastics Company Ltd.,
New Portland Street,
London, W.1.

1st January, 19..

Mr Miguel Reboles,
36 Plaza Orientale,
Buenos Aires.

Dear Sir,

The Directors of this Company decided at their last meeting to extend their activities to South America and to seek the services of an agent of established reputation in touch with the leading stores of Buenos Aires.

The representative of our bank has been good enough to send us your name and to assure us that through your extensive knowledge of South American trade and your wide connexion with leading firms you would be particularly suitable to undertake the work.

If you are willing to consider the acceptance of our offer, I shall be pleased to send you details of our products, their prices, and the conditions governing commission.

Yours faithfully,

for THE PLASTICS COMPANY LTD.,

Martin Shaw

Secretary

36 Plaza Orientale,
Buenos Aires.

12th January, 19..

The Plastics Company Ltd.,
New Portland Street,
London, W.1.

Sirs,

I have received your letter of the 1st January, and am indebted to you for your offer which I shall be pleased to accept, provided the terms of agreement are made satisfactory.

My business experience is wide and covers not only this city but the whole of the country. During the past fifteen years I have built up an extensive connexion with all the leading stores and, although I have not previously handled plastic goods, I have little doubt but that they will make an instant appeal to many of my clients. Given the best quality, together with reasonable prices and wide advertisement, I feel that I can be of considerable assistance to you.

One matter is of paramount importance, namely the necessity for stating clearly the nature and merits of the goods in Spanish as well as in English. My knowledge of both languages will be at your disposal.

I await the details of the terms suggested in our business dealings.

Yours faithfully,

Miguel Rebolès

The Plastics Company Ltd.,
New Portland Street,
London, W.1.

20th January, 19..

Mr Miguel Reboles,
36 Plaza Orientale,
Buenos Aires.

Dear Sir,

We thank you for your letter of
the 12th January, and are pleased to
note that our proposition appeals to
you.

We are sending you a number of
samples of our products, with a list of
prices and the terms upon which we are
prepared to commence trading. We shall
be prepared to pay a commission of 3
per cent on the value of all goods sold
and to make those payments monthly.

Our usual form of contract with
our agents in other countries is enclosed and we shall be glad if you will
sign and return it to us.

Yours faithfully,

for THE PLASTICS COMPANY LTD.,

Martin Shaw

Secretary

[R.S.A. S.T.C. Adv.]

F

SECTION V

EXPOSITION

A. SENTENCE STRUCTURE
B. PARAGRAPHING
C. PLANNING A WRITTEN COMPOSITION
D. EXERCISES IN PARAGRAPHING
E. EXERCISES IN DESCRIPTION
F. PRELIMINARY ESSAY EXERCISES
G. ESSAY TOPICS
H. REPORT-WRITING
I. MEMORANDA
J. EXERCISES IN REPORT- AND MEMO-WRITING

A. Sentence Structure

The sentence is the unit of prose expression and in its simplest form consists of a single idea or subject commented upon by a predicate:

> The parcel arrived.

The subject *parcel* is given a sense of motion by the predicate—the verb *arrived*. This can be given greater precision by the extension of the predicate:

> The parcel arrived to-day.

The adverb *to-day* limits the action of the verb to one particular time.

The subject of a *Simple Sentence* can be further developed by the addition of phrases:

> The parcel arrived to-day after being delayed several times during its rail journey.

The two phrases added give information about the parcel before its arrival.

In a *Complex Sentence*, the addition of subordinate clauses further expands the main idea, giving causes, results, comparisons, etc.

> Although the parcel arrived to-day there are still other items to come in before we can resume work.
> If the parcel arrives, we shall be able to resume work.
> We can resume work because the parcel has arrived.

By the use of conjunctions—forming a *Compound or Multiple Sentence*—further ideas can be introduced. Comparisons can be made and other parallel information related to the main subject.

> The parcel arrived to-day, and work will be resumed on the new project. (Compound Sentence.)
> (*A new idea—resumption of work—has been introduced.*)
> The parcel for which we have been waiting arrived to-day, and work on the new project, which has been postponed for over a week, can be resumed. (Multiple Sentence.)

Such variation of sentence structure enables the writer to express ideas of varying complexity, and the careful use of different structure relieves monotony. The position of the main idea in the sentence has an important effect upon expression. Where the main idea comes at the end of the sentence:

If the parcel arrives we shall be able to resume work

the sentence is *Periodic*, the emphasis being placed strongly on the condition *If . . . .*
When the sentence is changed to:

We shall be able to resume work if the parcel arrives

it is then a *Loose* sentence, the main idea introducing the sentence.

In general, the loose sentence is used for straightforward expression—letter-writing, technical exposition, narrative, etc. The periodic sentence is used mainly for imaginative prose, where it is capable of greater emotional expression. This is not, however, a hard and fast rule; sentence form always depends on the particular subject, and even technical exposition demands the use of periodic sentences for emphasis.

B. **Paragraphing**

The scope of a sentence is limited. The rhythm of reading and understanding requires change and movement, and, as the expression of an idea expands, the single sentence becomes too clumsy to deal with it.

Although the parcel arrived to-day there are still other items to come in before we can resume work, but if those other items do not arrive within the next few days there will be a serious disruption in our work, which will mean that many men will be idle and will suffer hardship, which will mean in the end that our business will deteriorate and our overseas customers will look elsewhere for their goods, a situation which will have a bad effect on our national economy.

This multiple sentence is long and clumsy, devoid of natural prose rhythm, and tending to obscure rather than to explain the meaning. The sentence obviously requires more definite breaks—a series of sentences forming themselves into the next unit of expression, the paragraph.

Although the parcel arrived to-day there are still other items to come in before we can resume work. If those items do not arrive within the next few days there will be a serious disruption in our work. Many men will be idle, suffering hardship and causing our business to deteriorate. Our overseas customers will look elsewhere for their goods, and the national economy will suffer.

The sentences are now built up into a paragraph in much the same way as they themselves are developed. The main idea is expanded by a series of sentences commenting upon the first. Notice how the first two sentences—periodic sentences—create an emotional effect—a warning—followed by sentences of plain statement.

The general construction of a paragraph is a main idea, expressed in a *Topic Sentence*, qualified and modified by dependent or parallel sentences. This method of development may take various forms:

(a) the simple and logical development of a single idea

(b) the development of part of an idea in conjunction with other paragraphs

(c) in scientific writing, the complete expression of an argument or description (this, to avoid interruption in the thread of thought or argument)

(d) as a unit of prose rhythm, with similar effects to those of short or long sentences

(e) as a unit of direct speech (a new paragraph introduces each new speaker).

Each paragraph should contain a topic sentence expressing the salient idea which is then developed in various ways of explanation or illustration. The following examples show some of the methods of developing a paragraph, but it is obvious that they will not always be used in a pure form. One usually develops paragraphs in a mixture of methods depending upon the idea to be expressed:

1. *By repetition.* (The idea contained in the topic sentence is expressed in a variety of ways to give added effect or detail.)

Fog everywhere. Fog up the river, where it flows among green aits and meadows; fog down the river, where it rolls defiled among the tiers of shipping, and the waterside pollutions of a great (and dirty) city. Fog on the Essex marshes, fog on the Kentish heights. Fog creeping into the cabooses of collier-brigs; fog lying out on the yards, and hovering in the rigging of great ships; fog dropping on the gunwales of barges and small boats. Fog in the eyes and throats of ancient Greenwich pensioners, wheezing by the firesides of their wards; fog in the stem and bowl of the afternoon pipe of the wrathful skipper, down in his close cabin; fog cruelly pinching the toes and fingers of his shivering little 'prentice boy on deck. Chance people on the bridges peeping over the parapets into a nether sky of fog, with fog all round them, as if they were up in a balloon and hanging in the misty clouds.

[*Bleak House*, by Charles Dickens]

By the skilful use of ellipsis (omission of the verbs), Dickens emphasizes the repetition. His details of description are no mere catalogue, but by a process similar to that of the ciné-camera, he brings his details gradually into close-up—an example of the technique of the professional writer.

2. *By illustration*

Speech is an important factor of our daily life. Our success depends upon skill in using the gift of speech and in listening to other people using that gift. Speaking and listening, mixed in suitable proportions make conversation, discussion, or argument. Our ability in this art enables us to gain information, enjoy friendship, win favours, bring others round to our point of view, or, briefly, to get what we want.

3. *By comparison*

There are underlying resemblances between the theatre and the battle-field. Both present a picture of conflict and high tragedy; both have their moments of comic relief. Their audiences, whether in the darkness of the theatre or the harsh light of reality, suffer vicariously the torments of the characters involved.

4. *By contrast*

Tradition can make or mar an organization. Followed slavishly, it can stifle progress and discourage initiative. Used to provide stability and continuity it can prove a sound basis for future progress.

5. *By negative definition*

That man is no fool where business is concerned. He has no time for slackness, no praise for money dishonestly gained. Although unassuming in appearance he has no trace of the 'stuffiness' which often marks the successful business man.

6. *By classification*

In our latest catalogue we give details of three new types of coke-boiler. First, the Minor, a small domestic boiler suitable for water-heating and for a heated towel-rail. Slightly larger, the Medfire will provide the added comfort of part central heating. Our third, and largest model, the Grandfire, ensures full and efficient house-heating, and can also be used for office or workshop heating.

7. *By formal proof*

The expense involved in extra advertising has been heavy, far outweighing the slight increase in profits over the past month. Despite a carefully organized presentation of the facts and advantages by means of several advertising media, the response has been poor. Replies to our circulars have been disappointing —even though one or two reasonable orders have been obtained —and the goodwill of the company may have suffered. *Our policy of quick expansion has been a dismal failure.*

You will notice from this paragraph that the topic sentence need not be the introductory sentence. Loose and periodic paragraphs may be used in the way that the equivalent sentence constructions are used. The topic sentence in the example could introduce the sentence, creating a formal atmosphere instead of the idea of climax.

8. *By particulars and details*

The sight of an old theatre programme. The vibrating note of a violin. Firelight flickering on cutglass in high-ceilinged rooms. The snatch of a partly-remembered ballad. Half-forgotten recollections etched more vividly with every resurgence of thought and emotion. *Memory, like a trail of gunpowder flaring at the touch of the senses.*

This method of development is normally restricted to literary expression where an attempt is made to simulate the disjointed quality of random thoughts and emotion.

C. **Planning Written Composition**

The first stages of composition are selection and arrangement. You should make quick notes of the material you intend to use, ensuring that the items chosen are relevant to the subject and that they can be dealt with in the time or space allowed. These items should then be arranged in logical order: in description of a process, this would mean the order in which the process evolves; in the report of some activity, the chronological order of events; in an argumentative essay, the logical steps in the establishing of the argument; in explanation, the stages from the simple to the complex.

The arrangement should then be broken down into a paragraph plan, with the paragraphs indicating the various stages of development. It is often helpful to think of paragraph indention as a mark of punctuation—a stronger break than the full stop, but still requiring some method of transition to the next paragraph. Before embarking upon the final composition, you should compose topic sentences for each of the paragraphs, bearing in mind the need for transition. This framework ensures unity of composition and means that you have such a control over your material that you should be able to write the last paragraph even before completing the first. In plain language, it means that you know what you are doing and where you are going.

The following is a rough plan of a description of cleaning and maintaining a typewriter—arranged in paragraph framework with topic sentences:

Care and Maintenance of a Typewriter

1. *A typewriter is an expensive and complicated machine which requires careful attention.*

    Often treated carelessly. Taken for granted. Treated as expendable. Benefits of correct touch and alignment. Careful attention means clean work with less effort, and with fewer major overhauls.

2. *There are simple rules for everyday care and maintenance.*

Removing dust with soft cloth or long-handled brush. Preventing rubber dust from falling into basket. Polishing chrome. Cleaning type basket and type faces. Use of a dust cover.

3. *The typewriter needs careful oiling as well as dusting.*

Fine oil with camel hair brush or needle. Joints and points of friction. Type-bar bearings less frequently. Not too much oil.

4. *Mechanical defects should be dealt with by an expert.*

Possible damage through inexperienced handling. Sources of trouble located quickly.

5. *Regular overhauls mean less trouble.*

Expert servicing every few years. Stripping and cleaning of the machine.

Concluding sentence:

Such treatment is wasted unless the typist continues to treat her machine with care.

With such a plan completed it should then not be difficult to write the final description. Remember that the important part of composition is the planning—the selection and arrangement of the material in paragraph form. The rest is the mechanical process of writing.

D. **Exercises in Paragraphing**

(*a*) Develop each of the following topic sentences by the method shown:

1. The work was hard and laborious. (*Repetition*)
2. Too much kindness is often worse than too little. (*Contrast*)
3. The plan was useless. (*Negative definition*)
4. He cannot be considered a successful salesman. (*Formal Proof*)
5. The sea is part of our heritage. (*Illustration*)

6. It is easier to fight than to argue. (*Contrast*)

7. You should never expect something for nothing. (*Negative definition*)

8. Admirers are like planets. (*Comparison*)

9. The customer is always right. (*Formal proof*)

10. We can offer three schemes of repayment. (*Classification*)

(*b*) Develop each of the following topic sentences by any method you consider suitable and write the name of that method at the end of the paragraph:

1. Ignorance is no excuse.

2. The journey was dull and monotonous.

3. Three things occurred to make him see the error of his ways.

4. There was no sense in his argument.

5. There can be no increase in wages unless production increases.

6. Labour relations are deteriorating.

7. Politeness, like gold, is a much sought-after commodity.

8. His actions over the previous three days had certainly been strange.

9. To write successfully one must have something to say.

10. His thoughts were confused.

11. What we may think to be great, history may reject as trivial.

12. The salesman descended upon us like a bird of prey.

13. It is better to travel hopefully than to arrive.

14. However much you may dislike him you cannot ignore him.

15. You cannot change human nature.

16. The floating of a company involves several legal processes.

17. The main driving force of man is curiosity.

18. He had suffered more than his fair share of troubles.

19. Explosives are not dangerous until you forget that they are.

20. It was a hot, humid day.

21. A policy of appeasement never brings real security.

22. There are lonely outposts on the frontiers of science.

23. Education is a process of preparation.

24. Redundancy is a dreaded word in the workman's vocabulary.

25. The smart secretary knows the real meaning of simplicity.

26. Proficiency is not always accompanied by efficiency.

27. Magic was the forerunner of Science.

28. There was a tense atmosphere in the room.

29. He lacks the courage of his convictions.

30. Wherever we find trouble we find a test of character.

E. Exercises in Description

Explain in clear and logical sequence the steps required in the following operations:

1. Making a local call from a public telephone.

2. The careful opening of a new book.

3. Returning and taking out a library book.

4. Preparing and serving a simple meal.

5. Deposit and withdrawal of money in a post office savings account.

6. Inserting and withdrawing paper from a typewriter.

7. Reinserting a sheet of paper in a typewriter and gaining correct alignment.

8. Changing a typewriter ribbon.

9. Routine cleaning of a typewriter.

10. Typing an envelope.

11. Setting out a typewritten letter.

12. Preparing a set of household accounts.

13. The correct method of fingering in typewriting.

14. The correct way of using a shorthand notebook.

15. Tracing and remedying the fault when a typewriter carriage moves sluggishly after the keys are pressed.

16. The operation of a particular filing system.

17. Obtaining copies of typewritten work by means of a rotary duplicator.

18. Typing from a dictation machine.

19. The preparation of a simple report.

20. Preparations for a formal committee meeting.

F. Preliminary Essay Exercises

1. The following essay frameworks contain the topic sentences of the paragraphs together with brief notes. From these compose and write short essays.

(a) *The Cathedral*

(i) *The delicate spire soared above the houses, pointing past the clumsy factory chimneys.*

Contrast with modern industry and the smoke and grime of the city. Seems to be slowly crushed by the growth of the city, yet it is immediately noticeable and still dominates its surroundings.

(ii) *The smooth green lawns, the dark yews, and the smooth, weathered stones cut it off from the buildings around.*

The calm isolation of the cathedral. Absence of traffic in immediate vicinity. Orderliness, bulk, and strength.

(iii) *Over the massive doorway mediaeval figures paraded in a strange mixture of the beautiful and the grotesque.*

A close view of the carvings. Saints and devils. Facial expressions. Skill of the mason's chisel. A symbol of the passing from one age into another.

(iv) *In the cool, dark interior the silence could be felt.*

The sudden absence of time and the importance of meditation. The loss of contact with the outside world.

(b) *Emigration*

(i) *In the early stages of history man was a wanderer.*

The primitive nomad. Hunters moving after the herds. Inter-tribal warfare and pressure to move on. The gradual spreading of the world population.

(ii) *Even with the growth of settled habits man was still restless.*

The adventurous spirits. Explorers and warriors.

(iii) *Persecution and oppression drove men to other lands.*

>The Pilgrim Fathers, the Huguenots, etc. The strong feeling for liberty.

(iv) *The modern emigrant is stirred by similar causes.*

>Economic pressures. Need for liberty. Over-population. The urge to seek new worlds.

(*c*)   *Meetings*

(i) *A meeting is the coming-together of several persons for the discussion of items of common interest.*

>Constitution of a meeting. Authority to convene. Need for a quorum.

(ii) *The business of an organization is normally carried on by a small elected committee.*

>Election at A.G.M. Regular committee meetings. Purpose of Extraordinary General Meetings.

(iii) *Meetings require that sufficient notice be given to the members.*

>Date, time, and place. Time allowed for submission of proposed resolutions. Responsibility of Secretary.

(iv) *The notice of a meeting is usually accompanied by the agenda.*

>List of items to be discussed. Prevents items being overlooked. Keeps members to the point. Conventional lay-out of the agenda.

(v) *The Chairman conducts the business of the meeting.*

>His duties. The handling of proposed resolutions and amendments. Putting these to the vote. Closing of meeting when business has been completed.

2. In the following essay plans only the topic sentence for each paragraph is given. Make rough notes of the material for the development of these sentences, then write an essay. *Compose the last paragraph first,* going back to complete the others, until you have a finished, unified essay.

(a) *Rates and Taxes*

(i) Before communities were organized, people had to repair their own roads and provide their own protection.

(ii) A system of levying rates enables the local authority to provide amenities.

(iii) On a larger scale, taxation enables the government to provide nation-wide services.

(iv) Where the services overlap, government grants are made to supplement the money obtained from rates.

(v) The citizen's responsibilities are divided just as his interests are divided between his home neighbourhood and his country.

(b) *Is Television a Social Menace?*

(i) Once we used our imaginations, now we have them used for us.

(ii) Television is the great enemy of conversation.

(iii) If we do not think for ourselves, we shall soon be unable to judge for ourselves.

(iv) Television can broaden our minds and our interests.

(v) Intelligent viewing tends to encourage rather than discourage reading.

(vi) Television has the potentialities of a social menace unless it is used with discrimination.

(c) *Laughter*

(i) Laughter has many sounds and forms, and a multitude of moods behind it.

(ii) It can be a release from fears and tensions.

(iii) There is a hurtful note in some people's laughter.

(iv) The hypocrite can laugh with his mouth but not with his eyes.

(v) True laughter is complete and is the outward sign of happiness.

(d) *Interviewing*

(i) With its direct method of obtaining information or opinions, the interview serves many purposes.

(ii) An interview may be formal or informal.

(iii) The modern method tends to be a combination of the formal and informal.

(iv) The success of any interview depends largely on the personality of those interviewing.

(v) Remember that the person interviewed is the focal point of any questions and discussion.

(e)   *The Duties of a Receptionist*

(i) First impressions are important, and the receptionist must study her own appearance and that of her surroundings.

(ii) She must be ready to deal tactfully with any callers.

(iii) The telephone plays an important part in her daily work.

(iv) She must have an efficient memory and filing system.

(v) In all these duties she must, above all, consider her employer.

G. Essay Topics

1. The Age of the Ball-pen
2. Choosing a Job
3. Food from Tins
4. Labour-saving Machines in the Office
5. Mass-production
6. What makes an Office Comfortable to Work in?
7. The Advantages and Disadvantages of a Telephone
8. Contemporary Art
9. The Welfare State
10. The General Usefulness of Shorthand
11. Time-and-motion Study
12. The Need for a Simplified Spelling
13. Civilization and Noise
14. The Strangest Character I have known
15. The Fascination of Maps
16. Export or die
17. The Desire for Security
18. The Tyranny of Fashion
19. The Decline in Craftsmanship
20. Is Typing encouraging Slipshod Handwriting?

21. Are Educational Visits Worthwhile?
22. The Ideal Ingredients for a Summer Holiday
23. Newspapers and Public Opinion
24. Red Tape
25. Dropped Aitches
26. Which sport would you like to excel at, and why?
27. State-subsidized Art
28. Motives and Incentives
29. A Liberal Education
30. Snobs
31. The Vogue of Jazz
32. Attracting Tourists to Britain
33. The Use of Reference Books
34. T.V. and Mental Blindness
35. Two Characters in Search of a Story
36. The Ideal Boss
37. What makes the Smart Secretary?
38. Is the Education of Women a Waste of Time?
39. Overtime
40. The Art of Relaxation
41. Buying One's Experience
42. The Attraction of a multiple store
43. Is Advertising Necessary?
44. Monday Morning
45. "All the world's a stage"
46. The Dictatorship of the Box Office
47. The Three R's
48. The Real Meaning of Efficiency
49. Money
50. The Modern Miss
51. The Advantages of a Bank Account
52. The Fascination of Fair-grounds
53. "Leisure without books is death and burial alive"
54. The Importance of being Earnest
55. Washing-up
56. Monopolies
57. Things Taken for granted
58. Houses—to buy or rent?
59. Waiting-lists
60. Holidays with Pay

61. Social Misfits
62. The Dangers of Specialization
63. Misunderstanding in the Modern World
64. The Waste-paper Basket
65. Local Gossip
66. New Cinematic Techniques
67. Contemporary Furnishings
68. The Uses of Glass
69. The Stock Exchange
70. The Fight against Disease
71. Emigration as a Solution of the Population Problem
72. The Advantages of working for a Large Firm
73. Town Planning
74. Modern Air Travel
75. The Importance of Environment
76. The Search for Happiness
77. The Effects of Fussiness
78. Cruelty and Human Nature
79. The Art of Letter-writing
80. Filing
81. The Illusion of the Theatre
82. The Case for Local Government
83. Censorship
84. White Lies
85. The Refugee Problem
86. Organizing a House-warming Party
87. The Joys and Terrors of the Sea
88. Boots and Shoes
89. The Need for Utopias
90. Interior Decoration in the Office
91. Public Utilities
92. Crossword Puzzles—Game or Nightmare?
93. The Essentials of a Happy Home
94. "No man is an island unto himself"
95. The Employer-employee Relationship
96. The English Character as a Product of the Weather
97. The Importance of Concentration
98. Day-dreams
99. Responsibility
100. The Trials and Tribulations of Essay-writing

H. Report-writing

Whatever the size of a report—whether it be a single typed sheet or a massive printed volume complete with appendices and index—its purpose is the same: to convey information on a particular subject to a specific person or authority, or to a general audience.

Ordinary Reports

These pass on routine information—facts, figures, etc.—*e.g., reports of sub-committees to the main committee at regular meetings; monthly financial, progress, or sales reports.*

The reports are usually submitted at regular intervals without being specifically asked for, and the form they take is established by custom. Nowadays, a large proportion of such reporting is done by the filling in of specially-designed forms, and there is little basic variation from year to year.

Special Reports

These are composed for a specific purpose—*e.g., reports on fires and accidents, personnel reports, results of experiments and inquiries.*

The contents of such reports are decided by the *Terms of Reference*—*i.e.,* the instructions given by the person asking for the report. All the facts and arguments must then be carefully arranged in logical order—making sure that each point is completely relevant to the terms of reference—and the conclusions drawn from the facts clearly shown. At the end of the report recommendations are made in the light of the facts discovered.

The arranging of the material in such a form not only gives the person asking for the report a clear picture of the situation, but enables him to decide on the right course of action.

The outline of a Special Report is roughly as follows:

(*a*) Terms of Reference
(*b*) Steps taken in collecting information
(*c*) Presentation of the facts
(*d*) Conclusions drawn from the facts
(*e*) Recommendations

Composing the Report

  (*a*) The study of the objective—*e.g.*, the Terms of Reference
  (*b*) The collection of the facts
  (*c*) The arrangement of the facts in logical order, followed
     by the conclusions and recommendations
  (*d*) The outline plan—selection of section headings
  (*e*) Rough draft
  (*f*) Editing of rough draft, and writing of final report

A separate paragraph is required for each stage of the report (sometimes several paragraphs to cover one stage), the divisions being marked by sub-headings or marginal headings. The report should be headed and dated, and signed by the person making the report. Sometimes it is composed in letter form, but long reports are usually arranged in a more formal manner.

A personal report may be written in the first person, but many authorities object to this and require the report to be impersonally written in reported speech.

The important point to remember is: What is the report for and who will read it? Do not:

  (*a*) try to show your erudition
  (*b*) give unnecessary detail and irrelevant material
  (*c*) give unnecessary and confusing figures
  (*d*) spoil your strong arguments by adding weak and
     unnecessary ones
  (*e*) say what is *not* to be done unless specifically asked to
  (*f*) show your bias or prejudice.

Remember that a report requires: accuracy, conciseness, logical arrangement, correctness of grammar and style, and—above all—interest.

Example of a Short Report

REPORT OF THE HOUSING COMMITTEE ON THE DEVELOPMENT OF GRAYS MEAD ESTATE

Terms of Reference   In accordance with a resolution passed at the Main Committee Meeting held on the 12th April, 19.., the Housing Committee was instructed to examine the possibility of building a housing estate on the plot of land known as Grays Mead.

Proceedings   The Housing Committee met on three occasions
of the   —the 16th April and the 10th and 16th May—
Committee   and reports were received from their solicitor and
surveyor. Various members of the Committee
visited the site and submitted their findings at
the final meeting.

Findings   (*a*) The site is suitable for the construction of
two-storey houses. Main services are already
available and a negligible amount of levelling
will be required.

(*b*) There are no restrictive covenants on the
land, but the provisions of the local by-laws
require that the building line be set back
eighteen feet from the present roadway.

(*c*) The shape of the site precludes the building
of more than fifteen houses.

Conclusions   The maximum number of houses which can be
built on the site is fifteen, and this may prove
uneconomic in view of the capital expenditure
involved.

Recommenda-   (*a*) That the Main Committee should determine
tions   the maximum grant available for building.

(*b*) That the cost of building be investigated by
provisional tenders.

(*c*) That such cost be considered in relation to
the estimated income over the next ten-year
period.

Paul Smith
19th May, 19..   Chairman

I. **Memoranda**

A memorandum is a short informal message or report in
which the salutation and full signature of the letter form is
omitted. It is usually written on a specially printed memorandum form.

MEMORANDUM

From: To:

    The Manager, ...
      Smith and Jones Ltd., ...
        High Street, ...
        Milham.   ....

Date:............................   Subject:....................................

Short memos may deal with appointments or with routine inter-departmental business, but longer memos may be required where detailed information or recommendations are to be made without the formality of a report. For example, a memo is normally sufficient when a secretary is asked to collate and submit certain facts quickly to her employer.

In general, the method of compiling a report applies equally to the composition of a memorandum. Paragraphing is important and sub-headings may be used.

J. Exercises in Report and Memo writing

In the following exercises, presentation is more important than content. Your answers should be given in about 200 words.

1. Write a short report suggesting improvements which could be made in the design of your kitchen.

2. Make an objective report on your own progress so far in your course of study.

3. Report on the facilities available in your typing-room and suggest any improvements which could be made.

4. Report on an annual College function, assessing its success and recommending any alterations for the following year.

5. As Social Secretary of a Tennis Club you have been asked to make an annual report to be given at the A.G.M. The report is to deal with the previous year's activities and with the future of the section.

6. The testing of a new type of washing-machine has produced unfavourable results. Report on the tests giving a clear and balanced statement of the facts, and suggesting how the faults can be remedied.

7. As the representative of a firm of publishers you are sent to investigate the poor reception of a new book in the provinces. Submit your report giving the reactions of booksellers and customers and the conclusions you came to.

8. Your firm, owing to a drop in sales, is considering a new advertising campaign, but wishes to be sure that the moment is ripe for it. Submit a memorandum setting out the arguments for and against. Choose any manufactured article you wish, but consider carefully the nature of the article, public demand, seasonal demands, etc.

9. Your company proposes to open a branch office in another part of the country. Write a memorandum to your employer showing how this can be done successfully within three or four months.

10. Submit a report to your employer showing how the handling of incoming and outgoing mail can be improved.

11. Your firm has decided to open a training school for its apprentices, and has been offered a large building with extensive grounds for the purpose. You have been instructed to inspect the building and to comment upon its suitability. Make your report.

12. Your employer wishes to modernize the office. Submit a memorandum showing how this can be achieved with the minimum of capital expenditure.

13. Your employer has agreed to stagger the working hours in the firm to ease transport difficulties. Submit a memorandum showing how this can be done.

14. As the person in charge of a typing pool, submit a report on working conditions stressing several improvements which you consider to be long overdue.

15. A recent fire on your office premises proved to be the result of inadequate precautions. Make a report to the manager

detailing the existing fire precautions and the extra provision which must now be made.

16. A piece of waste land next to your office building is to be developed by your firm. The board has suggested using it for additional office premises, as a car park, or to develop a new business interest. Submit a report on its suitability for each purpose and make your recommendations.

17. As the person in charge of a small office you have been asked to provide information about one of your employees who is being considered for promotion. Make your report stating clearly and impartially the character, qualifications, etc., of the employee.

18. Your firm, manufacturing cosmetics, has decided to exhibit its latest products at a trade fair. Submit a memorandum giving details of the space available and recommending the form the display should take.

19. There have been several incidents of theft in your office. Draw up a report of these incidents and the action you have taken.

20. As the person in charge of a small branch of a large retail business, you have been asked to explain a rapid decline in sales. Make your report.

SECTION VI

REFERENCE AND PRACTICAL WORK

A. SOURCES OF INFORMATION
B. EXERCISES IN REFERENCE WORK
C. PRACTICAL OFFICE EXERCISES
D. PROOF-CORRECTING

A. Sources of Information

Facts are important. They form an integral part of commercial life, from the information needed to address an envelope to the facts about production asked for by a board of directors. "What were the terms of our contract with Mr X?" "How soon can we expect delivery of goods from Mr Y?" "Is there a branch of Mr Z's company in Leeds?" The experienced secretary should have such information immediately available, either from memory or from an efficient filing system. She is expected to be a mine of information—but that does not mean that she must cram her mind with a large number of extraneous and often irrelevant facts. She must learn by effort and experience what information is essential to the daily running and efficiency of the office; if a solicitor's office, the bias will obviously be towards legal terms and material; if an engineer's, a knowledge of the particular technical vocabulary and routine will be necessary.

The secretary will quite often meet queries and problems that are outside the normal routine, and she may have to answer them quickly. This means that she must know where to look for facts, and should realize that most of them are collected into books of reference—a formidable array of volumes, but so arranged that there should be no difficulty for the experienced searcher. Certain of the general reference works should be available in the office, but she will have to refer to local or specialist libraries for the specialist books. A telephone call to the library concerned should produce helpful advice—librarians are invariably keen to help those searching for information.

The golden rule of fact-finding is:

Refer to the general reference book first.

If the detail given there is insufficient, the reader will be guided to a more specialized work.

These other rules may be helpful:

(*a*) Make sure you know the difference between *Contents* and *Index*.

(b) Learn how to use an index properly. Do not 'flip' desperately through the reference book, but find out how the material is arranged. Use that arrangement to save time and labour, and be prepared for centre indexes, special sections, etc.

(c) Practise the quick method of referring to an alphabetically arranged book. It is surprising how many people waste time thumbing slowly and meticulously over the early sections of a dictionary when the word they want is much further on. Open the book approximately at the middle pages, and flick the pages through at speed with your thumb, moving in the appropriate direction and watching the sample words or roots given as guides at the top of each page.

(d) Learn to search for alternative classifications in an index. If you are looking for information about Filing, you may not find it in the index under that heading—it may be entered as a sub-section under Secretarial Duties.

The following books would provide a useful small reference library in the average office:

> *Concise Oxford English Dictionary*
> A shorthand dictionary
> A dictionary of abbreviations
> *Whitaker's Almanack*
> *The Post Office Guide*
> *The Typist's Desk Book*
> *The Office Desk Book*
> Railway and other timetables
> Telephone directories
> The appropriate *Kelly's Directories*
> *Titles and Forms of Address*

GENERAL REFERENCE BOOKS

The lists given below comprise merely a small part of the vast array of reference books available, but should be useful for average requirements. The use of these books will introduce you to the technique of searching for facts, especially if you study the structure of the books with care.

1. *Encyclopaedias*

The Encyclopaedia Britannica	
Chambers's Encyclopaedia	Alphabetical
The Everyman Encyclopaedia	
Pears' Cyclopaedia	16 Sections

For authoritative and detailed information refer to the standard works, the first three in the list. *Pears' Cyclopaedia* is a useful single volume work, divided into sections such as Gazetteer, Prominent People, Important Events, etc.

2. *Words*

> Oxford English Dictionary
> Foreign and bi-lingual dictionaries
> Fowler's *Modern English Usage*
> Fowler's *King's English*
> Roget's *Thesaurus of English Words and Phrases*
> Partridge's *Dictionary of Abbreviations*
> Benham's *Book of Quotations*

Fowler's two books give sound advice on the writing of English. The M.E.U. is alphabetically arranged; *King's English* is arranged in chapters dealing with particular problems of syntax, style, etc.

Roget's *Thesaurus* is a collection of synonyms and antonyms, of words and phrases. The arrangement of its sections seems complicated at first, but there is a good index.

3. *Places*

> The University Atlas
> Chambers's World Gazetteer
> The Statesman's Year Book
> Kelly's local and county directories
> Baedecker guides
> Railway, air, and shipping guides

The Statesman's Year Book has four main sections: International, Commonwealth, U.S., and Other Countries. It gives details of constitution, area, and population; there are commercial details and some statistical information.

Kelly's county directories give information about local

history, topography, village churches, etc. There are equivalent
volumes for cities and large towns. The local street directories
give lists of residents by roads and classified lists of trades.

The A.B.C. guides are alphabetical, and the information
about rail travel is restricted to main services, with suburban
timetables appended. Bradshaw's railway timetable is more
detailed, but more difficult to use. Both firms publish air
guides monthly.

4. *People*

> *Dictionary of National Biography*
> *Who's Who*
> *Debrett's* or *Burke's Peerage*
> *International Who's Who*

The full D.N.B. was originally in sixty-three volumes, this
formidable number being reduced to twenty-one in recent
years. There is, however, a concise D.N.B., which should serve
the average reader. It is divided into two alphabetical sections
—one for those living until 1900 and the second for the period
1901–40.

Who's Who deals briefly with prominent contemporaries in
this country—information about life, education, work, hobbies,
etc. There are specialist versions: *Who's Who in the Theatre,
in Literature, in Art,* etc., and details of distinguished people in
other countries—*Who's Who in Canada, in Australia, in America,*
etc., *Qui Etes Vous?, Wer ist's,* etc. Certain of the entries are
found in the *International Who's Who*.

5. *Events*

> *Keesing's Contemporary Archives*
> *Whitaker's Almanack*
> *The Annual Register*
> *The World Almanack*

Keesing's is a cumulative record of world affairs, well indexed
and kept up to date by news pages sent to subscribers to file
in a loose-leaf binder. The information is sent weekly, and is
divided into sections under country headings and subject
sub-headings.

Whitaker's Almanack is the most useful of general reference books, and should really be repeated under each of the headings. It gives much information about people and places—the peerage, M.P.s, certain government officials and departments; geographical and astronomical information; facts about the commonwealth and foreign countries. It is published annually and gives summaries of the events of the preceding year in science, literature, politics, etc. There is information about sports records, banking, insurance, hall marks, abbreviations— a list which these few items barely suggest. Whitaker's has a contents list and a good index at the front of the book.

The Annual Register surveys the year's events in four sections —U.K., Commonwealth, Foreign, and a section dealing with art, finance, law, trade, etc.

The World Almanack is an American equivalent of *Whitaker's*, but with a bias towards American information.

Special Reference Books

Many of the following books will be in constant use in particular firms and organizations, but may be of little general interest.

1. *Literary*

> *The Oxford Companion to English Literature*
> *The Oxford Companion to the Theatre*
> *Brewer's Dictionary of Phrase and Fable*
> *The Author's and Writer's Who's Who*
> *The Writer's and Artist's Year Book*

2. *Engineering*

> *Kempe's Engineer's Year Book*
> Technical dictionaries and handbooks
> *Jones's Engineering Encyclopaedia*

3. *Legal*

> *Law List*
> *Stone's Justice's Manual*
> *Osborn's Concise Law Dictionary*
> The various indexes to Acts, Statutes, etc.

4. *Financial and Economic*

> *F.B.I. Register*
> *Ministry of Labour Gazette*
> *Stock Exchange Year Book*
> *Directory of Directors*
> *Bankers' Almanack and Year Book*
> *Insurance Blue Book*

5. *Political and Social*

> *Municipal Year Book*
> *Hansard*
> *United Nations Year Book*
> *Annual Abstract of Statistics*

THE POST OFFICE GUIDE

One of the most useful day-to-day reference books in the office. It explains the services provided by the G.P.O.: Inland and Overseas mail; letters, parcels, telegrams, cables, radio telephone, teleprinter, savings, licences, premium bonds, etc. Details of charges are given, and information about prohibited articles, customs and export duty, etc.

The secretary should be aware of the Post Office services, especially those lesser-known methods of rapid communication —the Railex and other express systems. They are useful in an emergency.

B. **Exercises in Reference Work**

1. In which reference book(s) would you expect to find the following information?

(a) names of holders of the V.C. who are still alive
(b) information about premium bonds
(c) details of council building for the previous year
(d) the number of deaths in the U.K. for a particular year
(e) the value of a particular country's exports or imports

2. What useful information could you obtain from the following reference works?

(a) *The Ministry of Labour Gazette*
(b) *Willing's Press Guide*

(c) *Crockford's Directory*
(d) *Stubb's Directory*
(e) *Lloyd's Register*

3. Where would you look for the following information?

(a) a list of companies manufacturing a certain article
(b) instructions for sending a telegram overseas
(c) brief information about hall marks on silver
(d) lists of householders in a particular area
(e) the salutation and complimentary close for a letter to a Bishop
(f) the name of the M.P. for a particular constituency

4. Refer to *Whitaker's Almanack* for the following information:

(a) the address of the Burmese Embassy in London
(b) the measurements of Super Royal drawing paper
(c) the M.P. for Birkenhead
(d) the Town Clerk of Canterbury
(e) the address of the Royal Society of Arts
(f) the name of the President of Chile
(g) the population of Bermuda
(h) the central office of the Ministry of Fuel and Power
(i) the gross tonnage of the liner *Ile de France*
(j) the holder of the world athletics record for the men's 3,000 metres

5. Refer to the *Post Office Guide* for the following information:

(a) the maximum size of a post card
(b) the standard rate of charge for radiotelegrams
(c) the poundage on a five shilling postal order
(d) the British stamps that are still valid
(e) the minimum charge of a telephone call to France
(f) conditions for sending foodstuffs
(g) the *Railex* system
(h) how to dial or ask for an overseas telephone call
(i) the Business Reply Card service
(j) how to cash a telegraphic money order

6. Answer the following questions by referring to appropriate reference books:

(a) What does *op. cit.* signify?
(b) What is the French equivalent of Welsh Rarebit?
(c) What is the currency of Kuwait?

(*d*) What is the address of your nearest office of Customs and Excise?

(*e*) What is the frequency of air services from London to Paris, and what cheap rates are available?

(*f*) Where is the island of Leros?

(*g*) Who said: "Party is the madness of the many, for the gain of a few."?

(*h*) What is meant by the abbreviations—c.i.; pH.?

(*i*) What is the meaning of the law term *consensus tollit errorem*?

(*j*) Which is the nearest railway station to Lansdowne Way, London, S.W.8?

(*k*) Who is the British Agent and Consul in Tonga?

(*l*) For whom is the periodical *Die Hards* published?

(*m*) What is the correct use of the word *mutual*?

(*n*) What is meant by a Bottomry-Bill?

(*o*) Where was Thomas Gray, poet, educated?

(*p*) When were sixpences first coined?

(*q*) Who were the persons involved in a famous meeting at Ujiji, on 28th October, 1871?

(*r*) What is meant by the word *marrying* when used by (i) the builder, and (ii) the film technician?

(*s*) What is *miniver*?

(*t*) What are the chief imports of Thailand?

7. Refer to the appropriate guides and timetables for the following information:

(*a*) The distance by rail from Shrewsbury to Paddington. When is early-closing day in Shrewsbury?

(*b*) When does the steamer leave Mallaig for Stornoway, and what is the first class return fare for the journey?

(*c*) The route by British Railways from London to Stockholm.

(*d*) You wish to travel on a Thursday morning from Paddington to Hereford. The train must have a refreshment car. What trains are available?

(*e*) What air services are available from London to Hongkong?

(*f*) You intend travelling from Guildford, Surrey, to Stowmarket, Suffolk, and wish to arrive at about 7.30 P.M. Plan your rail journey.

(*g*) What is the time of the last Tube train from Holborn to South Kensington on a Sunday?

(*h*) The supplementary charge for a first class single-berth sleeper from London to Carlisle.

(*i*) You wish to travel from Croydon to Perth, on a weekday,

G

arriving at approximately 7 P.M. Give details of trains and connexions.

(*j*) Your employer intends to travel from London to Dublin. Plan his journey by rail or air, for him to arrive on a Thursday morning.

C. Practical Office Exercises

The following exercises involve certain aspects of English and reference work as applied to office routine. Read the instructions carefully, then write or type the letter, report, memo, etc., that is required, using appropriate reference books. Describe any other action you would take.

1. Act upon the following note left by your employer:

Miss X. I wish to see the appropriate official of Tenterden Council in connexion with the building of a new branch in that area. Combine it, if possible, with a visit to Mr. Thomas, our representative there, on 14th and 15th March. I have not booked an hotel. Please arrange and inform Mr. Thomas.

2. Your employer is busy preparing a speech he is to deliver at a luncheon. He asks suddenly for a quotation on the power of the Press. Supply one from the appropriate reference book.

3. Take action on the following note:

Gone to emergency meeting at Surbiton branch. Will be late for conference at Brighton. Send telegram of apology to Secretary.

4. Your employer says that he wishes to make a telephone call to America. How do you arrange this for him?

5. Take action on the following note:

Miss X. Shall be out of London next week, visiting our branch offices at Dorchester and Weymouth on Tuesday and Thursday respectively. Inform managers concerned, arrange accommodation and give me details of suitable trains.

6. As secretary in a solicitor's office you are asked to submit a memo giving a list of reference books you need for general use.

7. The General Manager telephones. He has found on his desk certain important documents which the Sales Manager

should have taken with him to a meeting about 100 miles away. The Sales Manager has already left by the 9 A.M. train to be in time for the meeting that evening. What action will you take?

8. As Secretary of the Staff Social Club you have been asked to arrange a Staff summer outing. You know that most of the members like a quiet, inexpensive day by the sea. Submit a short report to the committee, giving details of possible trips in your area.

9. Take action on the following note:

Miss X. I have arranged for a duplicator, three filing cabinets, and two typewriters to be transferred to our new branch office. Confirm this with the branch and arrange for transport of the equipment.

10. Mr. P. Gregg, Mr. A. R. Jolly, and Mr. M. Peake have been interviewed by your employer for a post in junior management. Your employer asks you to inform Mr. Jolly that he has been accepted for the post of Sales Manager in the Hereford area. You are to send suitable letters to the unsuccessful applicants.

11. Act on the following note:

Miss X. Have heard that Miss Y is ill in hospital. Draft a letter, for my signature, wishing her well and reassuring her about the work here.

12. Your employer, wishing to assess staff reaction to the new canteen, has asked you to submit a tactfully designed and worded questionnaire for his approval and for eventual circulation to all employees.

D. Proof-correcting

There are certain agreed symbols for correcting typewritten or printed material, a form of 'shorthand' which enables a printer to alter the type-setting with the minimum of trouble. Proof-correcting is involved in three stages of the preparation of printed matter.

Proof-correcting Signs

Sign in Margin	Mark in Text	Meaning
⊙ ⊙	left/ Then he	Insert full stop, colon
,/ ;/	You/sir, can	Insert comma, semi-colon
ˀ	the man/s	Insert apostrophe
ˀ ˀ ˀ ˀ	/This,/he said,	Insert inverted commas
ℒ	It is ~~is~~ not	Delete; take out
stet	over ~~the~~ way	Let it remain
□	came quickly. ⌐When he saw	Indent
fresh/	a/start	Insert matter in margin
⌣	the͜ir help	Close up
ℒ	tho∮se people	Take out letter and close up
‖		Straighten uneven margin
=	this was not	Straighten lines
⌃	AGENDA	Raise lines
↓	AGENDA	Lower lines
centre	CONTENTS	Put in middle of page or line
⅃	⅃When he saw⅃	Bring matter to left
Ⅎ	ΓWhen he saw	Bring matter to right
#	there/was not	Insert space
eq #	he ⌊is no fool	Make equal spacing

Sign in Margin	Mark in Text	Meaning
space out	<u>CONTENTS</u>	Spread words or letters further apart
N.P.	he came. [The new	Begin new paragraph
run on	what they saw.⌐ They did	No new paragraph
caps	CON<u>T</u>ENTS	Capitals
s. caps	<u>CON</u>TENT	Small capitals
l. c.	He Was not there.	Lower case
trs.	evidnet He [not] [was] there	Transpose
/-/	the swimming/pool	Insert hyphen
/—/	uncles, aunts, nephews/all were. .	Insert dash
d/	He dis/ not return	Replace letter(s)
that he gave false evidence	It is not true/	Insert further material
italic	It was a <u>faux pas</u>	Put in italics
# >	I. *Purpose* >It is intended..	Space between lines or paragraphs
⊃	I hap no idea...	Turn inverted letter right way up
⊥	came next. Then...	Push down space
×	to what purpose	Broken letter(s)
(?)	(Underline the doubtful section)	Doubtful material. Is it correct or suitable?
w. f.	Why Not. .	Wrong fount. Insert correct type face.

(a) *The Typed MS.*

This must be corrected in preparation for the initial printing stage. The style of type, the margin surrounds, etc., must be decided and noted on the MS.

(b) *The Galley Proofs*

The typewritten material is now set up in type, and this is placed in a tray known as a *galley*, and *pulls* are taken on inferior paper. These galley proofs are then proof-read, the appropriate symbols being used.

Example of Proof-correcting

TAYLOR AND PERKINS
LIMITED   *centre*

A year of achievement   *caps*

THE NINTH ANNUAL General MEETING of   *s. caps*
Taylor and Perkins Limited was held on   *trs.*
October 15 at Fordwich Herts, Mr F. A.
Perkins, the chairman, presiding. The
following extract is from the circulated   *#*
statement:

cap. the period covered by this report has been   *o/*
one of great achievement with trading profits   */a*
trs. and productivity the at highest they have   ×
× ever been.

run on Prospects are consequently bright for this
company, and we seem to be over the lean   *#*
years.

,/ We have during the period under review,   */iew*
l.c. Made every endeavour to cut manufacturing
may/ costs so that we remain in the export
market. This report—presented, remember   *,/*
at a time of general financial strain should   */—/*
reveal the success of that move.

(*c*) *The Page Proofs*

The galleys, which are printed on long sheets of paper without regard to pages, are now divided and the type set up in pages. *Pulls* are then given the final examination and correction before the matter is printed on the better-quality paper.

The vital stage of proof-correcting is in the examination of the typewritten MS. Alterations to printed matter can be very expensive, especially when material has to run over to a new line. The galley and page proof stage should involve merely the correction of printing errors—wrong fount, broken and inverted letters, etc.

The list of proof-correcting signs given in this section follows as closely as possible the general method in use, but there are variations, such as $\wedge$ instead of $\diagup$; the main aim is to avoid too many marks in the text. Make your margin symbols as clear as possible.

You can practise proof-correcting by using the symbols for marking your own typewritten work.

APPENDICES

A. SPELLING RULES
B. LINE-END DIVISION OF WORDS
C. ROMAN NUMERALS
D. PUNCTUATION
E. POINTS TO LOOK FOR IN SENTENCE CORRECTION
F. GLOSSARY OF ENGLISH TERMS

A. Spelling Rules

1. *i* before *e*, except after *c*, when the sound is *ee*.

 achieve receive piece
 Except: seize

2. Words ending in single *e* drop the *e* before *-able*, except when it is required to soften *c* or *g*.

 love—lovable
 notice—noticeable manage—manageable

3. Words ending in vowel and single consonant double the final consonant before adding *-ed*, *-ing*, *-er*.

 sin—sinner run—running
 can—canned

But the consonant is not doubled when there is no stress on the final syllable.

 profit—profiting benefit—benefiting
 Except: worship—worshipping

4. When the word begins with *s*, the *s* is retained after *mis-* and *dis-*.

 misspelling dissolve

5. When *all*, *full*, *till*, and *well* are used to form compound words they usually drop one *l*.

 well—welfare skill—skilful
 full—fulfil   until careful
 Except: farewell well-being

6. Verbs ending in silent *e* drop it before *ing*.

 state—stating mate—mating
 Except: seeing shoeing tingeing dyeing singeing hoeing eyeing

7. Nouns formed from adjectives ending in *-ate* usually change to *-acy*.

 accurate—accuracy private—privacy

8. Words ending in *y* preceded by a consonant change *y* to *i* when a syllable is added.

> lady—ladies   rely—relied

9. Words ending in *y* preceded by a vowel are unchanged when a syllable is added.

> Chimney—chimneys   allay—allayed

> *Except:* money—monies

10. Words ending in *-our* usually drop *u* before *-ation*, *-ize*, *-ate*, and *-ous*.

> vigour—vigorous—invigorate
> valour—valorous

11. In words ending with silent *e* the *e* is usually retained before a suffix beginning with a consonant.

> care—careful   bore—boredom
> hire—hireling

> *Except:* argument truly duly awful nursling wisdom wholly
> —and the alternatives: abridg(e)ment judg(e)ment acknow-
> ledg(e)ment

B. Line-end Division of Words

This routine part of the typewriting technique usually causes more trouble than seems necessary, but it must be mastered if any speed and accuracy is to be gained. The setting up of words in print allows for much greater freedom than in a typescript, where certain 'rules' must be observed. The following is a list of suggestions for such division, together with a definite set of rules for occasions when words are not to be divided.

1. In words ending in *-ing*, divide before the *-ing*.

> deceiv-ing   discern-'ng   avert-ing

2. When the final consonant is doubled before *-ing*, divide between the two consonants.

> regret-ting   shop-ping   (*But:* distress-ing)

3. Divide before *-sion, -tion, -cian*.

deriva-tion   occupa-tion   proces-sion   physi-cian

4. Divide before *-tial, -cial*.

residen-tial   offi-cial

5. Divide before a suffix of *more* than two letters.

fellow-ship   compart-ment   capab-ility
disput-able   spine-less   separ-ate

6. Divide after a prefix of *more* than two letters.

com-mittee   over-hear   trans-lation
mis-construe   intro-duction

7. Where there are two consonants between two vowels, divide between the two consonants.

oppor-tunity   main-tenance
obser-vant   deben-ture

8. Where there are three consonants between two vowels, divide after the first consonant.

frus-trated   infil-trate

9. Divide between two vowel sounds (unless a diphthong), or after the first vowel when followed by a diphthong.

continu-ous   retali-ation   circu-itous

10. Where the above suggestions do not apply, divide according to syllables.

atti-tude   prelim-inary

In general, try to divide according to the sense of the words, if possible keeping enough of the whole word on the first line to imply the meaning. Note that several of the words in the above examples can be divided in more than one way—*e.g.*, com-mittee *or* commit-tee.

Never divide:

(*a*) for a proper noun
(*b*) for one or two letters at the beginning or end of a word
(*c*) short words of two syllables

(*d*) at the end of three consecutive lines
(*e*) in legal documents
(*f*) words of one syllable and their plurals
(*g*) on the last line of a paragraph or page
(*h*) in the middle of figures
(*i*) between initials of names

C. **Roman Numerals**

I	II	III	IV	V	VI	VII	VIII	IX	X
1	2	3	4	5	6	7	8	9	10

XI	XV	XIX	XX
11	15	19	20

XXI	XXIV	XXV	XXIX	XXX
21	24	25	29	30

XL	L	LX	LXX	LXXX	XC	XCIX	C
40	50	60	70	80	90	99	100

CC	CD	D	DCC	CM	M
200	400	500	700	900	1,000

EXAMPLES

44	XLIV
96	XCVI
190	CXC
1324	MCCCXXIV
1863	MDCCCLXIII
1953	MCMLIII

D. **Punctuation**

1. *The Comma*

The most important mark of punctuation for the correct communication of meaning. Constant practice is the only sure way of mastering the use of the comma but the following notes should give some guidance in the more obvious uses.

(*a*) To separate adjectives preceding a noun.

He was a poor, unfortunate, misguided individual.

But the commas may be omitted when monosyllabic adjectives are used.

> He was a poor old man.

(*b*) To separate words or phrases in apposition.

> Mr Jones, a member of the local council, was asked to preside.

(*c*) After the nominative of address.

> Jones, you will take the other route.
> Dear Sir,

(*d*) To separate words or phrases in a series.

> Nails, screws, tacks, glue, and wood were needed.
> The rattle of harness, the creaking of saddle leather, the clip-clop of hooves, created a martial atmosphere.

(*e*) To separate short co-ordinate clauses in a compound sentence.

> He walked down the road, but she did not see him.

(*f*) Parenthesis, or interpolation in direct and indirect speech.

> He argued, quite rightly, that the feat was impossible.
> "This," he said, "is what I consider to be true."

(*g*) To separate adverbial phrases and clauses from the main clause.

> The door being locked, he could not get in.
> In cases of burglary, where personal property is involved, a more serious view is taken.

(*h*) To separate noun and adjective clauses where they occur in groups.

> He knows what to do, how to do it, and the best time for it to be done.

(*i*) To show ellipsis.

> He will reach the top; you, never.

(*j*) After a preposition used as an adverb.

> Below, the sea stretched out before them.

(*k*) To mark a parenthetical or non-defining clause.

My neighbour, who is an interfering busybody, causes much trouble.

(*l*) In large groups of figures requiring separation into groups of three.

17,000   146,000   13,000,000

(*m*) After an absolute phrase.

The man having shown his ticket, the collector let him through the barrier.

(*n*) In the date, between month and year.—*e.g.*, 13th January, 19.., 16th March, 19..

2. *The Full Stop*

(*a*) To indicate the end of a sentence.

We have now received your order.

(*b*) After initials and abbreviations.

A. R. Smith   S.W. 19.
D.S.O.   Capt. Brown

N.B. Where an abbreviation ends in the same letter as the original word the full stop is not obligatory (e.g., *yd* or *yd*., *pd* or *pd*.), but it is customary in business letters to use a full stop after Mr. Co. Ltd.

(*c*) In numerical indications of time, to separate hours and minutes—*e.g.*, 10.20 A.M.

(*d*) In a series of stops to show omission of word(s).

Brown's book points out, "The history . . . is one of unrelieved barbarity."

(*e*) As leaders—usually in tabular work—to guide the eye.

G. Mason	...	...	...	...	15.6 seconds
A. Brown	...	...	...	...	16.3 seconds
E. Smith	...	...	...	...	15.4 seconds

(*f*) In typing, to indicate the decimal point—*e.g.*, 24.6

(It is Continental practice to use the comma to indicate the decimal point.)

N.B. A full stop is not necessary:

(i) at the end of a heading, unless it ends with an abbreviation
(ii) after words and figures used in tabular work (except decimal points, separation of money, etc.)
(iii) after what seem to be abbreviations but are really symbols: 1st, 2nd, 3rd; 4to.

3. *The Semicolon*

(*a*) Separating co-ordinate clauses, especially when there is no conjunction.

> The land is sterile, the house has fallen into disuse; there is little use in my reclaiming the farm.

(*b*) To show antithesis.

> Your work is talented; his is the work of a genius.

(In strong antithesis the semicolon may be replaced by a colon.)

(*c*) To give a suitable pause in a lengthy sentence in which commas have already been used.

> Man is heir to many ills, and he staggers through life the dreary victim of tiny germs often of infinitesimal size and holding the power of sudden death; yet he is never completely subdued by their threat.

4. *The Colon*

(*a*) To introduce a speech or a quotation.

> The speaker said:
> As Smith once said:

(*b*) To introduce a statement added in explanation or as an afterthought.

> Old people are useful to the community: they often provide a storehouse of wisdom and experience.

(*c*) The colon, or a colon and dash (:—), is used to introduce a list (often after such expressions as *as follows, thus, the following*). There is no definite rule as to the use of one particular form, but usually the colon and dash serves a more formal purpose, especially when introducing a list that begins on a new line.

> We have the following items: pens, pencils, books, and rulers.
> We wish to order the following items:—
> > 4 doz. tins of fruit salad
> > 3 doz. tins of apricots

5. *The Dash*

(*a*) In parenthesis.

> The new member—a man of some wit—took his place on the platform.

(*b*) To indicate interruption in direct speech.

> "What we want is—oh, never mind."

(*c*) To show omission of a name or of figures.

> They stopped at the town of —— in 19— (or 19..).

(*d*) To show hesitancy of speech.

> "I am—well—er—should be—sorry."

(*e*) To gather a scattered subject.

> Bells, organs, whistles, sirens—all united in the cacophony of welcome.

(*f*) At the end of a quotation, before the name of the author or source.

> "Music can soften pain to ease."—Pope.

6. *The Hyphen*

(*a*) To connect parts of a compound noun.

> swimming-pool   night-watchman

(Some such words have become permanent compounds—*e.g.*, *notebook, eyewitness*.)

(*b*) To join the words in a compound adjective.

> a two-foot rule   rag-and-bone man

(*c*) To show syllabic division of a word.

> beau-ti-ful   dark-ness

(*d*) As an alternative to the diaresis when two vowels are to be sounded separately.

coöperation   *or*   co-operation

(*e*) To differentiate words of the same spelling but different meanings.

recover/re-cover   recreation/re-creation

(*f*) Between the tens and units in numbers written in word form.

nine hundred and thirty-six

(*g*) After certain prefixes.

ex-President   neo-Platonic   pre-war

(*h*) To show division at line end (see the notes on page 202).

7. *Parentheses*

(*a*) Enclosing references to source, authority, definition, etc., of a foregoing statement.

The means of transport (*i.e.*, those set out on pp. 32 to 34 of the manual) are . . .

(*b*) To show alternative rendering of a sum of money.

We enclose the sum of £4 3s. (Four pounds three shillings) in payment of . . .

(*c*) To enclose figures or letters used with sub-headings and in enumeration. The (*c*) at the beginning of this note is an example.

(*d*) In verbatim reports to show interruption.

"I see no reason why (*cries of "Resign!"*) this matter should not . . ."

8. *The Apostrophe*

(*a*) Shows the genitive, usually indicating the possessive, but idiomatically in phrases such as *a day's pay*. See section (*c*).

SINGULAR: add *'s*
         boy's book.   man's destiny.
         a year's work
     But: for goodness' sake

PLURAL: add '

      two years' work   ladies' shoes

  But: men's shoes

In some proper names, *'s* is added where it might seem unnecessary—*e.g.,* St James's Square; Dickens's Books.

In compound nouns, the apostrophe usually follows the last word—*e.g.,* the men-servants' quarters.

(*b*) To show omission of letter(s) in a word.

    It's (It is)   'phone (telephone)

(*c*) In nouns denoting time and space.

    a hard day's work   three weeks' holiday

(*d*) To show the plural of certain symbols and letters which are not normally pluralized.

    Mind your p's and q's.   He won two 1st's.

9. *Capital Letters*

  (*a*) At the beginning of a sentence.

  (*b*) For proper nouns.

    January   Victoria plums

(*c*) For titles of books, plays, etc. The first word always begins with a capital letter, and all other words, except articles, prepositions, and conjunctions, have an initial capital letter.

    "The Times"   "The School for Scandal"

(*d*) In personification.

    Can Honour's voice provoke the silent dust. GRAY

(*e*) At the beginning of direct speech, and at the resumption of direct speech when a new sentence begins.

    He said, "We are unable to come."
    "This is no use," he remarked. "We must try again."

10. *Inverted Commas*

  (*a*) Direct speech.

    "This is the way," he called.

(*b*) Quotation.

> According to Thomas Hobbes, "Leisure is the mother of Philosophy."

(*c*) For quoted titles.

> "Hard Times," by Charles Dickens is . . .

(*d*) For names of ships.

> H.M.S. "Ark Royal"

But: it is now more usual to italicize titles and names of ships. This can be indicated in a typescript by underscoring, or by a note in the margin.

(*e*) To indicate slang, and dubious words or phrases.

> He was very "cut up" about it.
> Smith's "theory" has received little support. (indicating that the writer doubts that it is a theory)

(*f*) Single inverted commas for quotation within quotation.

> "We have painted some of those signs marked 'No entry'."

Be careful about the position of other punctuation marks.

> "Have you read 'The Horse's Mouth'?"

11. *Brackets*

To show interpolation of word(s) not in the original passage quoted.

> I saw him [Edward White] early in 1921.

E. **Points to look for in Sentence Correction**

ERRORS OF GRAMMAR

Faulty Agreement

1. When the subject is separated from the verb by several words, phrases, or clauses:

> The collection of string, toffee papers and other odds and ends *were* emptied from the boy's pockets.

The subject is *collection*, a singular noun, therefore the verb should be in the singular—*was*.

(N.B. In some circumstances a collective noun can be used with a plural verb. The deciding factor is whether the collection is treated as a coherent whole or the emphasis is placed on the individuals forming the collection.)

The party of sightseers has lost its guide.
The party of sightseers have forgotten their sandwiches.

2. Confusion in the use of *and* and *with*.

The boy and his dog disappear into the forest.

disappear is a plural verb following a compound subject joined by the conjunction *and*.

The boy with his dog *disappears* into the forest.

Here *with* is a preposition introducing an extension of the subject *boy* which requires the singular verb.

3. Careless use of the relative pronoun which must agree with its antecedent in number and person and takes its case from its own clause.

He is one of the best runners who *has* raced on this track.

The relative pronoun *who* refers to *runners* and is therefore plural, taking the plural verb *have*. Similarly, errors of case can occur.

That is the person *who* the policeman stopped.

Who is the object, in its own clause, of the verb *stopped* and should be in the accusative—*whom*.

That is the boy who I believe was absent.

Who is in the correct case because it is the subject of the verb *was*.

But, N.B.: That is the boy whom I knew to be absent.

4. Mistakes of agreement occur frequently after *this, that, each, every, either, neither*, which are *singular*, and *these* and *those*, which are *plural*.

Those sort of things are not done *should be* That sort of thing is not done.

Each of the men did their duty *should be* Each of the men did his duty.

Neither of the pens are for sale *should be* Neither of the pens is for sale.

5. Parts of the verb *to be* and the conjunction *than* are followed by the same case as precedes them:

It was him   *should be*   It was he.
He is larger than me   *should be*   He is larger than I.

N.B. the difference between:

I like you better than him   *and*
I like you better than he (does).

Errors in the Use of the Verb

1. Wrong sequence of tenses.

(*a*) The tense of a verb in narrative must not be changed unnecessarily and illogically from present to past or vice versa.

(*b*) If the main verb of a sentence is in the past tense, the subordinate verbs must also be in a past tense. A main verb in the present tense may be followed by any tense.

He said that he *will* carry out the task.

Said is in the past tense, therefore the subordinate verb should be in the past—*would*.

2. A split infinitive should be avoided:

He tried to carefully avoid his friend.

Carefully splits the infinitive and makes a clumsy construction. The sentence should be written:

He tried carefully to avoid his friend.

N.B. In rare circumstances, where ambiguity could arise, there is some argument for breaking the rule, but it would then be advisable to recast the sentence.

3. The perfect infinitive is often used clumsily. There is some reason for writing:

He hoped to have met them.

This is a brief way of expressing non-fulfilment. But

I should have liked to have met them

involves clumsy repetition and could be written:

I should have liked to meet them.

4. Confusion between gerund and present participle. The gerund is a verbal noun, the present participle usually a verbal adjective.

He did not see him running.

In this sentence *running* is a present participle.

He did not hear of *him* running.

Here, *running* is a gerund and should be governed by the possessive adjective *his*, not used with the personal pronoun *him*.

5. Use of *shall* and *will*.

(*a*) Simple future: *shall*, 1st person; *will*, 2nd and 3rd persons.

(*b*) Expressing determination: *will*, 1st person. Expressing obligation, permission, or necessity: *shall*, 2nd and 3rd persons.

Comparison of Adjectives

1. The comparative is frequently used incorrectly.

He is more knowledgeable than any living man.

This indicates that he is not a living man and the sentence should read:

He is more knowledgeable than any other living man.

2. The superlative should not be used with the phrase *of any* . . .

It has the largest appeal of any radio show

should read

It has the largest appeal of all radio shows

or

It has a larger appeal than any other radio show.

The Use of 'like' and 'as'

1. *As* is a conjunction of comparison, corresponding to the adjective *like*.

He does not play the piano *like* I do.

Like is used incorrectly as a conjunction. The sentence should read:

> He does not play the piano as I do.

2. *Like* is used:

(*a*) as an adjective: *He is like his brother.*
(*b*) as an adverb: *He ran like a hare.*
(*c*) to introduce an adjective phrase: *His manner was, like his father's, abrupt.*

Double Negative

Although you will not commit the gross error of saying, "He don't know nothing," you are likely to fall into the trap in longer sentences.

> They realized that it was *impossible* to find amongst the ruins *scarcely* any trace of a clue.

SPECIFIC ERRORS OF SYNTAX

1. Careless positioning of pairs of conjunctions such as *both . . . and, neither . . . nor, either . . . or, not more . . . than.*

> He could both write poetry and prose

should be

> He could write both poetry and prose.

2. Ambiguity caused by incorrect positioning of an adverb.

> He needed his hair cutting badly

should be

> He badly needed his hair cutting.

N.B. the use of *only*. Different positions, different meanings:

> I *only* spoke to him.
> I spoke *only* to him.
> *Only* I spoke to him.

3. Misplacing of words, phrases, and clauses—which should be placed as near as possible to the part of the sentence they are intended to qualify or modify—can result in ambiguity.

> My uncle shot a bear *in his pyjamas.*
> She played records for those at sea *on the radio.*

4. Unrelated participles and relative pronouns.

Participles:

Walking through the town, the streets looked deserted.

Walking is a participle with no relation to the main part of the sentence—certainly not to the streets. The phrase it introduces can be changed into a subordinate clause:

As he walked through the town, the streets looked deserted.

Relative pronouns:

There were only two people at the meeting, *which* caused it to be postponed.

The relative pronoun *which* has no antecedent. One should be provided or the sentence recast:

The fact that there were only two members present caused the meeting to be postponed

or

The meeting was postponed because only two members were present.

5. Ambiguity through the careless use of pronouns:

Jack told Jim *he* was no use.

(*He* might refer to Jack or Jim.)
Be very careful in using the pronoun *it*.

ERRORS OF STYLE

1. Sentence structure—sentences too complicated; overuse of parenthesis; lack of variety in sentence structure; undue repetition of conjunctions and particular types of phrases or clauses.

2. Tautology—unnecessary repetition.

need not necessarily; strange phenomenon, final conclusion, joint partnership, etc.

3. Verbosity—an unnecessary abundance of words.

We are pleased to be able to inform you that at last a representative will be directed to proceed to your particular area, and that he will arrive some time during next month.

This could be simply expressed as:

We shall send our representative to your area next month.

4. Mixed metaphors. Avoid such obviously ludicrous mixtures as:

We have our backs to the wall and must therefore put our noses to the grindstone.

Some mixed metaphors are, however, less easy to notice.

His aim of becoming Prime Minister was crushed suddenly by his fall from favour.

5. Malapropism—the incorrect use of a word which bears a close resemblance to the word intended.

He has an *incredulous* (incredible) ability to resist most forms of *decease* (disease).

6. The ampersand (&) should be used only in business addresses and for certain technical material.

7. The colloquial forms *don't, I'll, he'd*, etc., are not used in written expression, except in dialogue or direct quotation.

Colloquialisms (words and phrases which are on the verge of slang) should be avoided in written expression.

What *ever* made him do that?
Where *on earth* did you *pick that up*?

Slang should, of course, be avoided.

8. Clichés and overworked words. Clichés have, in their time, been novel and effective but, by reason of constant use, have become stale. Their use in written expression can produce that same staleness. Avoid them.

Leave no stone unturned;   far be it from me . . .;
be that as it may . . .;   it stands to reason . . .;
the supreme sacrifice;   the height of folly.

Some words are overworked because they pander to mental laziness. In some instances they are used incorrectly:

nice, jolly, rather, pretty, aggravate, tremendous, terrible, awful.

9. Prepositions are sometimes used idiomatically, and for no apparent reason, after verbs and adjectives. This usage must be respected—*e.g., different from, absolve from, oblivious of*, etc.

9. Jargon. This term is properly applied to the sectional vocabulary of a particular science, profession, or trade, where special terms are necessary apart from the common pool of English vocabulary. The artist with his *chiaroscuro, aesthetic,* etc.; the radio mechanic with his *flutter and negative feedback*; the motor engineer with his *compression ratios*—each employs a special terminology to obtain economy of expression.

When this sectional vocabulary becomes bloated and ugly; when expressions are created almost for their own sake, jargon cannot be defended. An added danger is the spreading of such language into general English usage.

If it is ugly-sounding, difficult to understand, circumlocuitous, and pompous it can serve no useful purpose.

Civil Service jargon:

Members of the administrative staff are permitted to acquire the necessary forms by purchase through any one of the normal authorized channels.

Journalese:

An immense gathering of people congregated opposite Smith's store to watch an attempt to get the fire under control. Strenuous efforts on the part of the local fire brigade prevailed, and no one sustained serious injury.

Commercial jargon:

· We are the recipients of your favour of the 15th ult.

It is possible to translate each of these examples into English.

F. **Glossary of English Terms**

AFFIX. Addition made to the beginning or end of a word root. (See *Prefix* and *Suffix*.)

AGREEMENT. Shows the concord between one word and another in gender, number, person, or case; for example, between subject and verb, relative pronoun and antecedent, adjective and noun.

AMBIGUITY. The doubtful meaning of a sentence, arising from confused pronouns, misplaced phrases, clumsy punctuation, or double meaning of a word.

Tom asked Bill if he could go to the cinema.
When the Indians charged the settlers they were all killed.

ANTECEDENT. A noun, or noun equivalent, to which a following relative refers.

The *offer*, which contained more reasonable terms, was accepted.

ANTITHESIS. Arranging words in parallel to emphasize the contrast of ideas.

More haste, less speed.
The spirit is willing but the flesh is weak.

ANTONYM. A word of opposite meaning to another. *Valuable* has the antonyms *valueless* and *worthless*.

APPOSITION. The use of a noun or noun equivalent in conjunction with another to give added information or description.

Mr. Brown, *the butcher*, is a local councillor.
The fact *that he had failed* was obvious from his expression.

AUXILIARY VERB. A verb (such as *be, may, have, do*) which helps to form the different moods and tenses of other verbs.

He *has* gone home.
He *will* try.
He *may* do it.

CASE. That form of a noun, pronoun, or adjective which indicates its relation to other words in the sentence. As English is now largely an uninflected language—*i.e.*, it has lost most of its case endings, the problem exists only in the following:

(*a*) the genitive of certain nouns, mainly those denoting persons:

John's book; the men's shoes;

(*b*) the accusative, dative, and genitive of certain pronouns:

To *whom* did you give the book?
Whom did you see?
I met *him*.
I gave *her* the book.

CLAUSE. A group of words which contains a subject and a finite verb but is itself part of a sentence. It may be main, subordinate, or co-ordinate.

> *He is wise* and *he should know*
>   (Main)   (Main—co-ordinate)
> *what to do.*
>   (Subordinate)

CLICHÉ. Stereotyped phrase that has lost its original freshness and vitality:

> as like as two peas; to leave no stone unturned; between you and me.

COLLOQUIALISM. A word or saying that belongs to familiar and everyday speech, but which is usually out of place in formal written expression.

> won't, don't, etc.
> He couldn't care less.
> to pay through the nose.

DIAERESIS. A mark used to show that two vowels placed together in a word are to be sounded separately.

> coöperative (alt. co-operative)
> aërated

DIPHTHONG. The combination of two simple sounds to make a different single sound.

> *a* and *i*   make the single vowel sound in 'p*i*ne'
> *i* and *oo* make the single vowel sound in 'd*u*ty'
> *a* and *oo* make the single vowel sound in 'h*ou*se'

The combination of two vowels or two consonants to make a single sound is called a *Digraph*.

> *sh* in shirt
> *ea* in reach

ELLIPSIS. Syntactical shortening of sentence construction by omission. We often say that the missing words are 'understood.'

> That was the man (whom) we saw.
> Has he gone? He has (gone).

FIGURATIVE. Describes language which involves extensive use of figures of speech.

FIGURES OF SPEECH. Unusual methods of expression used to gain added emphasis or effect—*e.g.*, Metaphor, Simile, Irony, Synechdoche, Innuendo, etc.

FINITE. The finite forms of a verb are those which are restricted to a particular subject with which they agree in number and person:

He *takes* every opportunity.

GENDER. No longer exists in nouns, in the English language. There is gender, however, in certain pronouns—e.g., *he* (Masc.), *she* (Fem.), and *it* (Neuter); *who* (Masc. and Fem.) and *which* (Neuter).

GERUND. A non-finite part of the verb which may act as both verb and noun.

Balancing an account can be tedious work.
Balancing is the subject of the sentence and has its own object *an account.*

The gerund has the same ending (*-ing*) as the present participle, with which it should not be confused.

HOMONYMS. Words that are identical in form but have different meanings.

caddy—for golf or for tea?

HOMOPHONES. Words having the same sound but of different spelling.

aisle and *isle*; *read* and *reed.*

IDIOM. Peculiarities of expression which cannot be translated literally into another language.

He was told to *drink up.*
He likes being *in the limelight.*
She was ready *in less than no time.*

MALAPROPISM. Confusion of words which have a superficial resemblance, often with ludicrous results. (Name derived from Mrs. Malaprop in *The Rivals.*)

This meat is quite *indelible* (inedible).

METAPHOR. Transferring the significance of a word to a different context.

> The guns bombarded the city. (*literal*)
> He was bombarded with questions. (*metaphorical*)

NEOLOGISM. The coining of a new word, often for a specific purpose.

> Cinerama, feedback, quizmaster, etc.

NUMBER. The form of a word which denotes whether it is singular or plural.

PARENTHESIS. Something set apart from, or interrupting the normal construction of a sentence. It can be indicated by the use of commas, dashes, or parenthese*s* (small brackets).

> I have, as you know, had some experience.
> The residue (£400) will go to charity.

PHRASE. A collection of words, without a finite verb, acting as a noun, adjective, or adverb in a sentence.

> *Having finished,* he went home.
> He knows *what to do.*

PREFIX. An addition made at the beginning of a word, usually to alter its meaning in some way.

> hurt   *un*hurt
> pay   *re*pay

SIMILE. A likening of two things or actions to give greater clarity or effect. It normally consists of the comparison of two different things which possess only one striking resemblance.

> He was as white as a sheet.
> The Assyrian came down like a wolf on the fold.

N.B. the use of *like* or *as.*

SOLECISM. A blatant error of grammar, pronunciation, or even of etiquette.

> He asked if *you was* speaking the truth.

SUFFIX. An addition made at the end of a word, usually to alter its part of speech.

> help   help*ful* (noun to adjective)

SYNONYMS. Words of similar use and meaning. (N.B. the use of *similar*; each word in a group of synonyms usually has its own particular significance.)

work, task, job, duty.
compassion, sympathy.

TAUTOLOGY. An unnecessary repetition.

strange phenomenon, very unique, final conclusion.